Mark Cholij

English
Basics

Practice & Revision

CAMBRIDGE
UNIVERSITY PRESS

CAMBRIDGE
UNIVERSITY PRESS

University Printing House, Cambridge CB2 8BS, United Kingdom

Cambridge University Press is part of the University of Cambridge.

It furthers the University's mission by disseminating knowledge in the pursuit of education, learning and research at the highest international levels of excellence.

www.cambridge.org
Information on this title: www.cambridge.org/9780521648653

First published 1999
14th printing 2014

A catalogue record for this publication is available from the British Library

ISBN 978-0-521-64865-3 Paperback

Layout and composition by Newton Harris Design Partnership

Illustrations by Tim Sell

ACKNOWLEDGEMENTS
Thanks are due to the following for permission to reproduce from copyright material:
p. 78 from an article by Valentine Low in the London Evening Standard.
'The Lawyer and the Oyster' (p. 70) and 'The Stella' (pp. 71–72) appeared originally in Arthur Mee's Children's Encyclopaedia (Everybody's Publication Ltd., 1963).

Every effort has been made to locate copyright holders for all material in this book. The publisher would be glad to hear from anyone whose copyright has been unwittingly infringed.

Contents

Introduction

This book forms part of a three-stage series that aims to cover the 'mechanics' of the English language (spelling, punctuation and grammar) at three graded levels. The emphasis in each of the books is on practice and revision.

Each of the three books offers a systematic work and study programme for use in the classroom or at home. Book 3 revises and builds upon the material covered in Book 2.

As the final book in the series, Book 3 has been written specifically for students in the 14–18 age group. As a revision manual, Book 3 is also suitable for adults who wish to revise the general principles of English spelling, punctuation and grammar.

The book is equally suitable for students whose first language is not English. In broad terms, Book 3 is suitable for those students whose standard of English is at Cambridge Advanced level (CAE) or Cambridge Proficiency level (CPE).

Book 3 consists of thirty units, and each unit is divided into three sections. **Section A** consists of preliminary tasks which introduce the main topic and seek to establish the student's individual strengths and weaknesses. Having checked his/her answers to the preliminary tasks by referring to the key at the back of the book, the student is then directed to the **Reference** section. Having consulted the reference section, the student proceeds to **Section B** where the main topic is extended, revised and consolidated. A marking system is included in Section B for those students who wish to measure their progress.

Although the book is designed in such a way that one can dip in at random, it is recommended that students follow the order in which the units appear. This is especially important if the book is being used for individual study.

Glossary

Before starting this book, you should make sure that you are familiar with the following grammatical terms printed in bold:

1 The English alphabet has 26 letters, comprising five **vowels** (A, E, I, O, U) and twenty-one **consonants**.

2 A **verb** is a 'doing', 'being' or 'having' word (denoting action, occurrence, state or experience). The **subject** of a verb is the 'doer' of the action. The **object** of a verb is the 'receiver' of the action.

3 A **noun** is a word used to denote or name a person, place, thing, quality or act. A **compound noun** (e.g. rainfall) is a noun made up of two words or more.

4 A **pronoun** (e.g. he, she, it) replaces a noun.

5 An **adjective** describes a noun or pronoun. A **compound adjective** (e.g. good-looking) is made up of two words or more.

6 The primary function of an **adverb** is to tell us more about a verb (e.g. she *easily* passed the exam) or an adjective (e.g. it was a *really* easy exam). An **adverbial phrase** (e.g. all of a sudden) is a group of words that acts in the same way as an adverb.

7 Prepositions are words like *in*, *on*, *from*, *at* and *by* which are usually (but not always) found before a noun or pronoun.

8 Conjunctions are linking words such as *and*, *but*, *or*, *if* and *when* that are used to join other words, groups of words or parts of a sentence.

9 A **sentence** is a set of words complete in itself and grouped together in such a way as to make complete sense. In written English, a sentence begins with a capital letter and ends with a full stop, a question mark (?) or an exclamation mark (!).

10 A **clause** is a group of words containing a verb. The following sentence consists of two clauses: 'Although I am very fond of you, I don't want to marry you.'
In the sentence above, *I don't want to marry you* is the **main clause**.
A main clause can stand on its own as an independent sentence.
Although I am very fond of you is a **subordinate** (or **dependent**) clause.
A subordinate clause cannot stand on its own as an independent sentence.

11 Participles are verb forms used primarily in combination with the verbs *to be* and *to have* to form compound tenses. e.g. I am *eating*. (present participle) / I have *eaten*. (past participle)

1 Greek and Latin roots 1

A

Task 1

The following words in italics are Greek in origin:

tele = far off, at a distance; *phone* = sound, voice; *graph* = visual symbol (picture or written); *scope* = look at, observe; *micro* = very small

How many English words can you make from these Greek root words by combining one with another?

Task 2

a In Latin, the past participle of the verb *scribere* (= to write) is *scriptus* (= written). The Latin word for 'hand' is *manus*.

1 Which English word is derived from the combination of *scriptus* and *manus*?
2 What word do we use when we refer to 'cosmetic hand-care'?
3 Which adjective do we use when we refer to 'unskilled' labour?
4 What word do we use when we refer to the sacred writings of a religion?
5 In what contexts do we use the word 'script' in English?

b Here are three verbs: *inscribe, describe, prescribe*. Use the noun form of each of these verbs to fill in the gaps below.

1 The chemist could not make out the doctor's handwriting on the _____ .
2 We were moved by the _____ on the gravestone.
3 He wrote a very interesting _____ of his polar expedition.

Now check your answers and then consult the **Reference** section before going on to **B**.

Reference

a When we use the term *root*, we mean a word or word element from which other words are formed. Many English words take their roots from Greek and Latin words.

e.g. *auto* (Greek) = self / by oneself; *bio* (Greek) = life; *audio* (Latin) = I hear; *video* (Latin) = I see; *visus* (Latin) = sight

b We can build upon a root word in three basic ways:
  ● We can combine the root word with other root words.

e.g. biography, autobiography, autograph, videophone

- We can add a <u>suffix</u> (i.e. an addition placed at the <u>end</u> of the word).

e.g.   audible, audience, audition, visible, vision, phonetic

- We can add a <u>prefix</u> (i.e. an addition placed at the <u>beginning</u> of the word).

e.g.   inaudible, invisible, revision

NB Many of our most common prefixes and suffixes are also Greek or Latin in origin.

c Recognising the function and meaning of the most common root words, prefixes and suffixes will help your spelling, increase your vocabulary and develop your reading comprehension skills.

B

Task 1

A number of English words are derived from *dictus*, the past participle of the Latin verb *dicere* (= to say). How many English words can you think of that either begin with or end with the root element *dict*?

Score: one mark per word

Task 2

From the Latin verb *cedere* (= to go), we have *-ceed* and *-cede*.

1 Fill in the gaps below with these three verbs: *receded, proceeded, preceded*.

a He then _____ to lecture me on my behaviour.
b The main event was _____ by a fireworks display.
c Once the tide had _____ , we found that we could reach the island on foot.

2 Each of the verbs you have just used has a prefix. Which prefix means 'before'? Which prefix means 'back'? Which prefix means 'forward/on'?

3 Use *-ceed* or *-cede* to complete the definitions below.

a to ex_____ : to go beyond a permitted limit
b to con_____ : to admit (that something is true)
c to suc_____ : to come after somebody (in time) / to achieve an aim

4 Only one word in the English language ends in *-sede*. Do you know the word? Clue: the first part of the word is a prefix beginning with *s-*.

Score: /10

Greek and Latin roots 2

* *

A

Task 1

From the Latin verb *trahere* (= to draw, in the sense of 'take' or 'pull') and its past participle *tractus*, we have the root element *tract*. Hence, a 'tractor' is a vehicle that *pulls* farm machinery. Look carefully at the following words (each formed with a prefix + *tract*) and place each one where appropriate in the gaps below: *attract, contract, detract, distract, extract, retract, subtract.*

1 He was forced to _____ his allegations.
2 We were able to _____ a lot of information from the text.
3 She had to _____ one number from another.
4 The new shop found it very hard to _____ business.
5 We should not allow his present behaviour to _____ from his past achievements.
6 Do not _____ the driver while the bus is moving.
7 He refused to sign the _____ .

Task 2

Answer the following questions:

1 What can an *ambidextrous* person do?
2 What do we mean when we say that a statement or message is *ambiguous*?
3 If you have an *ambivalent* attitude (or *ambivalent* feelings) towards someone or something, what does that mean?
4 What is the general meaning of the root word *ambi*?

Now check your answers and then consult the **Reference** section before going on to **B**.

Reference

a A knowledge of root words is particularly useful when dealing with specialised/academic vocabulary. e.g. What is 'polygamy'? What is 'monogamy'? What is 'bigamy'? (Clue: *gamy* = marriage; *poly* = many; *mono* = one; *bi* = two.)

Polygamy is the custom of being married to more than one person at the same time. British law only allows monogamy (being married to one person). If you are married and then marry another person, you are committing the crime of bigamy (being married to two people at the same time).

b When looking up the meaning of a difficult word, it is always worth checking to see what root words are involved.

B

Task 1

What do the underlined words mean?

Tigers and wolves are <u>carnivores</u>. Cows are <u>herbivores</u>. We are <u>omnivores</u>.

Score: /3

Task 2

The root word *cide* means 'killer/killing'. Complete the definitions (1–5) by selecting from the words given. You will not need to use all the words.

suicide/homicide/herbicide/pesticide/fratricide/genocide/matricide/ patricide/infanticide

1 _____ : the extermination of a whole race or nation.
2 _____ : the crime of killing one's father.
3 _____ : the act of killing oneself.
4 _____ : murder (the killing of another human being).
5 _____ : a chemical used by farmers and gardeners to destroy weeds.

Score: /5

Task 3

Choosing from the words given, add a suitable prefix or suffix to each uncompleted word below.

anti (= against), *arch* (= main, chief), *fore* (= before, ahead), *hyper* (= too/extremely), *phobia* (= fear or hatred of), *pseudo* (= false, pretending to be …), *retro* (= backward/s)

1 Everybody in the team felt despondent when they were beaten 2-0 by their _____ *-rivals*.
2 You're just talking _____ *-intellectual* nonsense!
3 This material is _____ *sensitive* to light.
4 *Claustro* _____ is the fear of enclosed spaces.
5 In _____ *spect*, it is easy to see where we went wrong.
6 She claims that she can _____ *tell* the future.
7 He was arrested during the _____ *-war* demonstration.
8 Food additives can make children _____ *active*.
9 She can't stand spiders. She suffers from *arachno* _____ .
10 Not wishing to use her real name, she wrote the novel under a _____ *nym*.
11 He argued that to adopt the policy would be a _____ *grade* step for the company, and that they would soon regret it.
12 Their victory was a _____ *gone* conclusion.

Score: /12

Loan words (words/phrases taken from other languages)

A

Match each 'loan' word (1–9) with its country of origin (*a–i*).

1 sauna 2 siesta 3 fjord 4 cuisine 5 kindergarten 6 cosmonaut
7 soprano 8 drama 9 karate
a France *b* Spain *c* Greece *d* Japan *e* Finland *f* Germany
g Norway *h* Italy *i* Russia

Certain abbreviations in English are Latin in origin. Translate the following Latin phrases into English:

Latin	Abbreviation		English
Anno Domini	AD	=	
ante meridiem	a.m.	=	
exempli gratia	e.g.	=	
et cetera	etc.	=	
id est	i.e.	=	
nota bene	NB	=	
post meridiem	p.m.	=	
post scriptum	PS	=	
Requiescat in pace	RIP	=	

Fill in the gaps below with the following French words: *cache, etiquette, faux pas, rapport, coup.*

1 The teacher established a good _____ with his class.
2 Unfortunately, troops loyal to the government were unable to thwart the military _____ .
3 He committed a terrible _____ at the dinner party when he made a crude joke at the expense of the hostess.
4 When the police raided the terrorists' hideout, they discovered an arms _____ in the basement.
5 In a finishing school for young ladies, social _____ is the core subject on the curriculum.

Now check your answers and then consult the **Reference** section before going on to **B**.

Reference

a Over the years, the English language has 'borrowed' many foreign words and phrases. Many of these 'loan' words are very common ones and usually cause no problems of comprehension.

e.g.   marmalade (Portuguese), ski (Norwegian), macho (Spanish), hamburger (German), algebra (Arabic)

Quite often, however, a common 'loan' word may be tricky to spell.

e.g.   yacht (Dutch); yoghurt (Turkish); graffiti, paparazzi, ghetto, confetti, spaghetti (Italian); psychology, hippopotamus, pseudonym, synonym, pneumonia, phenomenon, catastrophe (Greek)

b Some words which come from other languages have special plurals.
- <u>Greek</u>: crisis - crises; hypothesis - hypotheses; oasis - oases; criterion - criteria; phenomenon - phenomena
- <u>Latin</u>: cactus - cacti (*or* cactuses); formula - formulae (*or* formulas); fungus - fungi (*or* funguses); medium - media; nucleus - nuclei (*or* nucleuses); radius - radii (*or* radiuses); stimulus - stimuli; vertebra - vertebrae (*or* vertebras)
- <u>French</u>: bureau - bureaux (*or* bureaus); chateau - chateaux (*or* chateaus); gateau - gateaux (*or* gateaus)

NB From the point of view of style, it is preferable to use the original Latin and French plural forms rather than the anglicised forms given in brackets.

B

Task 1   Correct the following words, which have been misspelt:

pnuemonia - fenomenon - catastrofe - hipopotamus - sicology - confeti - grafiti - spaggeti - getto - yogert   Score: /10

Task 2   Make the following nouns plural (without using *-s*):

chateau - stimulus - radius - fungus - formula - cactus - medium - criterion - crisis - oasis   Score: /10

Task 3   Explain the meaning of the Latin words used in the sentences below.

1 Some students were keen on reform, but the majority were happy to preserve the *status quo*.
2 We were not sure whether he was a *bona fide* student, so we asked for some form of identification.
3 They considered all the *pros* and *cons* very carefully before deciding to invest money in the project.   Score: /3

4 American/British spelling 1

A

Underline and change any examples of American spelling in the sentences below. Tick any sentence which is acceptable in British English.

1　She was upset by her neighbor's behavior.
2　Blue is her favorite color.
3　He bought a liter of wine.
4　He used his driving license as a means of identification.
5　As it was his first offense, he was let off with a warning.
6　She apologized when she realized her mistake.
7　Is there anything interesting in that catalog?
8　He grabbed an ax and killed the wolf.
9　There's an interesting program on TV tonight.
10　They say they have no plans to modernize the hotel.
11　He practiced medicine for ten years before he became a priest.
12　We need to get some more practise before the match.

Now check your answers and then consult the **Reference** section before going on to **B**.

Reference

Where differences exist between American and British spelling, the spelling in American English tends to be simpler.

Note carefully the following:

a　American (-*or*): e.g. behavior, color, favor, honor, neighbor
　　British (-*our*): e.g. behaviour, colour, favour, honour, neighbour

　　NB British English is not consistent and some nouns end in -*or* (e.g. horror, terror).

b　American (-*er*): e.g. center, fiber, liter, meager, somber, theater
　　British (-*re*): e.g. centre, fibre, litre, meagre, sombre, theatre

c　American (-*se*): e.g. defense, license (noun), offense, practise (noun)
　　British (-*ce*): e.g. defence, licence (noun), offence, practice (noun)
　　American (-*ce*): e.g. practice (verb)
　　British (-*se*): e.g. practise (verb)

　　NB With certain words in British English, we indicate the noun form with a *c* and the verb form with an *s*.

e.g.　to practise, to advise, to devise, to license / a lot of practice, a piece of advice, a device, a licence

d American: a computer program, a TV program
British: a computer program, a TV/theatre/social programme

e American: ax, catalog, dialog
British: axe, catalogue, dialogue

f American (-*ize*): apologize, modernize, realize
British (-*ize*/-*ise*): apologize/apologise, modernize/modernise, realize/realise

NB Except for a few words like *advertise*, *advise*, *devise*, *supervise* and *surprise*, it is entirely up to you whether to use -*ize* or -*ise*. Although dictionaries tend to favour -*ize*, it is more practical to use the -*ise* form. Just over a hundred years ago, the -*ize* form was prevalent in British English. Nowadays, however, the simpler -*ise* form is equally popular.

B

| Task |

Underline and change any examples of American spelling in the sentences below. Tick any sentence that is acceptable in British English.

1 The trouble with him is that he has no sense of humor.
2 It was an honor to meet such a distinguished person.
3 We rarely go to the theater these days.
4 He said that he sympathized with her.
5 How much does your country spend on defense?
6 The students were penalized for poor spelling.
7 They are not licenced to sell alcohol.
8 He played tennis badly because he was out of practise.
9 She practises the piano every evening.
10 He came to school in a multicolored jacket.
11 He supplemented his meager wages by working as a barman in the evenings.
12 The film has a lot of action and very little dialog.
13 They live in a rough neighborhood.
14 She asked for directions to the town center.
15 This year's results compare favorably with those of previous years.
16 She looked at him in horror.
17 He asked me for a special favor.
18 A mile is equal to 1.6 kilometers.
19 The knight wore a suit of armor.
20 It was a somber occasion and nobody smiled.

Score: /20

American/British spelling 2

A

Task

Underline and change any examples of American spelling in the sentences below.

1 Farmers usually start plowing their fields in the spring.
2 I didn't have any cash on me, so I paid by check.
3 She said that she had never traveled outside Europe.
4 My woolen jumper shrank in the wash.
5 She has gray hair and walks with a limp.
6 Our journey was delayed because the car had a flat tire.
7 The politician skillfully avoided answering any awkward questions.
8 The car accident left him totally paralyzed.
9 If you want to do that particular course, you need to enroll before 10 September.
10 We had a marvelous time at the party.
11 We were rather skeptical about their chances of winning the match.
12 Before the operation, he was given a strong anesthetic to put him to sleep.

Now check your answers and then consult the **Reference** section before going on to **B**.

Reference

In American English, certain words and combinations of letters are spelt as they are pronounced. Those same words and combinations of letters are spelt slightly differently in British English.

Note carefully the following:

a In each of the following pairs, the first word is British and the second word is American:
cheque / check; cosy / cozy; draught / draft; grey / gray; jewellery / jewelry; moustache / mustache; plough / plow; pyjamas / pajamas; sceptical / skeptical; through / thru; tyre / tire

b American (-*e*):

e.g.   anesthetic, archeology, encylopedia, hemorrhage

British (-*ae*):

e.g.   anaesthetic, archaeology, encyclopaedia, haemorrhage

NB It is also acceptable to write *encyclopedia* in British English.

c American (-*yze*):

e.g.   analyze, paralyze

    British (-*yse*):

e.g.   analyse, paralyse

d American (-*ll*):

e.g.   appall, enroll, installment, skillful

    British (-*l*):

e.g.   appal, enrol, instalment, skilful

e American (-*l*):

e.g.   dialed, equaled, instal, marvelous, traveled, traveler, woolen

    British (-*ll*):

e.g.   dialled, equalled, install, marvellous, travelled, traveller, woollen

NB Technically, *to install* is like *to forestall* and should end in -*ll*, but in practice it is often spelt with one *l* (*to instal*) in British English. Either form is acceptable.

B

Task   Underline and change any examples of American spelling in the sentences below.

1 She dialed the wrong number.
2 He didn't have a beard, but he had a mustache.
3 They spent two weeks analyzing the data.
4 There's a draft in here. Could you close the window?
5 Has anybody seen my pajamas?
6 He bought her some jewelry for her birthday.
7 Jaimini's father is a famous archeologist.
8 They are paying for the carpet by installments.
9 She spent two months traveling all around Europe.
10 We went for a walk thru the forest.
11 He was admitted to hospital with a brain hemorrhage.
12 On his second attempt, he equaled the world record.

Score: /12

6 Confusing words 1

A

Task

Complete each statement or question by selecting the correct alternative in brackets.

1 It made no difference. It didn't (affect / effect) us at all.
2 Owing to (averse / adverse) weather conditions, all flights were cancelled.
3 It was just an optical (allusion / illusion).
4 It was quite an (appreciative / appreciable) rise in price.
5 I'd like to (compliment / complement) you on your work.
6 The police have still not identified the (corps / corpse).
7 Have you got a spare (envelop / envelope)?
8 Many (eminent / imminent) scientists agree with her.
9 Who will stop the (elicit / illicit) trade in whale meat?
10 The escaped prisoner (eluded / alluded) capture for over a week.
11 There was an official (inquiry / enquiry) into the disaster.
12 His instructions were most (explicit / implicit). Why didn't you follow them?
13 They treated their prisoners in a (human / humane) way.
14 He is brilliant. He has come up with an (ingenious / ingenuous) solution to the problem.

Now check your answers and then consult the **Reference** section before going on to **B**.

Reference

Words that look alike are a major source of confusion when reading or writing English. Whenever in doubt, check the meaning and spelling of a word in a dictionary. Note carefully the dictionary definitions of the following words:

1 <u>to affect</u> = to produce an effect on / to make a difference to; <u>an effect</u> = result/consequence; <u>to effect</u> (e.g. a change) = to bring about / to accomplish / to put into effect
2 <u>averse</u> (to) = opposed (to); <u>adverse</u> = negative/hostile
3 <u>allusion</u> = reference; <u>illusion</u> = deception/delusion
4 <u>appreciative</u>: showing one's appreciation; <u>appreciable</u> = considerable/noticeable
5 <u>to compliment</u> = to praise; <u>to complement</u> = to complete / to combine well with

6 <u>corps</u> = select group; <u>corpse</u> = dead body
7 <u>to envelop</u> = to wrap up in / to cover closely on all sides;
   <u>an envelope</u> is used for sending letters
8 <u>eminent</u> = distinguished/famous; <u>imminent</u> = soon to happen
9 <u>to elicit</u> = to draw out; <u>illicit</u> = illegal
10 <u>to elude</u> = to avoid / to escape; <u>to allude (to)</u> = to refer (to)
11 <u>an enquiry</u> is a general request for information; <u>an inquiry</u> is an
   official investigation
12 <u>explicit</u> = clear/definite/open; <u>implicit</u> = implied (but not openly
   expressed)
13 <u>human</u>: relating to (or concerning) people; <u>humane</u> = kind / not
   cruel / merciful
14 <u>ingenious</u> = original/brilliant; <u>ingenuous</u> = innocent/naïve

B

Task

Look carefully at the sentences below. Tick those sentences that are
correct. Underline and correct any word that has been misused.

1 He's still suffering from the effects of the drugs he took.
2 The film had quite an affect on her.
3 The noise outside is effecting my concentration.
4 My grandmother is not averse to the odd gin and tonic.
5 The company has had a lot of averse publicity recently.
6 He is under the allusion that he is next in line for promotion.
7 It made a change to have such an appreciable audience.
8 There has been an appreciative drop in the number of
   students attending his class.
9 The workbook and cassette compliment the course book.
10 The President of the United States and his press corpse arrived
   early this morning.
11 The mountain was enveloped in mist.
12 They were warned that a strike was eminent.
13 The teacher found it difficult to illicit a coherent response
   from the student.
14 I recognise him, but his name alludes me.
15 During her speech, she alluded to the lack of co-operation she
   had received from certain members of staff.
16 Can you wait? I will make some enquiries.
17 Although he doesn't say so openly, his distrust of modern
   technology is explicit in everything he writes.
18 One cannot change humane nature.
19 Many people regard fox-hunting as inhuman.
20 It was rather ingenious of her to ask a complete stranger to
   look after her luggage while she went to buy a ticket.   Score: /20

Confusing words 2

A

As you read the text below, choose the correct alternative in brackets.

"Am I to (infer / imply) from what you are saying that you are dissatisfied with the way we manage things here?" asked Mr Rosinger in an icy tone.

"All I am saying is that (moral / morale) amongst staff is very low," replied Mr Atkins. "I merely wish to point out, most (respectfully / respectively), that we are all rather concerned about the lack of communication between management and staff – (especially / specially) with regard to certain changes in the office. For instance, we no longer have free (access / excess) to the (stationery / stationary) cupboard. Nobody, however, has told us why. This breakdown in communication is most (regrettable / regretful) and we feel that something must be done about it."

Mr Rosinger grunted, blew three rings of cigar smoke into the air and then asked very quietly:

"Is that your (principal / principle) grievance, Mr Atkins?"

"Of course not. However, I am (loath / loathe) to discuss this matter any further without other members of staff being present. Could we not arrange for a formal meeting to take place between management and staff, perhaps with someone (disinterested / uninterested) in the chair?"

Mr Rosinger chewed slowly on his cigar.

"Would you like my reply now or (later / latter)?" he drawled.

"Now, please."

"(You're / Your) fired!"

Now check your answers and then consult the **Reference** section before going on to **B**.

Reference

Note carefully the following:

1   to imply = to hint (to state something indirectly); to infer = to deduce (to draw a conclusion from what has been stated)
2   morale: a general feeling of confidence / enthusiasm / determination; moral (adjective): relating to standards of good or bad behaviour / fairness / honesty, etc.
3   respectfully = politely; respectively = in the order stated

4 <u>especially</u> = in particular; <u>specially</u>: refers to something done for a particular purpose

5 <u>access</u>: means of approaching or entering a place / opportunity to use or approach somebody or something; <u>excess</u>: too much of something

6 <u>stationery</u> (noun): paper, envelopes, things for writing; <u>stationary</u> (adjective) = not moving

7 <u>regrettable</u>: to be regretted / describing something one regrets (e.g. a regrettable mistake); <u>regretful</u>: feeling or expressing regret (e.g. a regretful shake of the head)

8 <u>principal</u> (adjective) = main / chief / primary; <u>principle</u> (noun): a basic idea / belief / doctrine; <u>in principle</u> = in theory

9 <u>loath</u> (or <u>loth</u>) = unwilling / reluctant; <u>to loathe</u> = to detest / to hate

10 <u>uninterested</u> = indifferent / not interested; <u>disinterested</u> = impartial / unbiased

11 <u>later</u>: the comparative form of *late*; <u>the latter</u>: the second of two people or things already mentioned

12 <u>you're</u> = you are; <u>your</u>: possessive (e.g. your book)

B

Task

Correct any errors in the sentences below. Tick any sentence that is correct.

1 He implied from her comments that all was not well.
2 The unexpected victory boosted the team's morals.
3 In the 200 metres and the 400 metres, Fergus came first and third respectfully.
4 She shrugged her shoulders and gave me a regrettable smile.
5 The boat was especially constructed to withstand arctic conditions.
6 It is easier to hit a stationery target.
7 He said that he was disinterested in politics.
8 He won't do it. He says it's against his principals.
9 You'll have to pay for any excess luggage.
10 She's loathe to admit that she is in the wrong.
11 It sounds fine in principal, but will it work in practice?
12 Does this store have a stationary department?
13 It is your morale duty to help her.
14 What are you inferring? Are you calling me a liar?
15 Becky, Gillian and Hazel were dressed in pink, blue and yellow respectively.
16 Package holidays, specially to Spain and Greece, are much cheaper than they were last year.
17 We stock plastic chairs and wooden ones, but the later are rather expensive.

Score: /17

Words that sound alike

A

Underline and correct any spelling mistakes in the sentences below.

1 I was very surprised when she walked straight passed me without even saying hello.
2 I wasn't sure weather he was joking or not when he said he was going to wring my neck.
3 The frail old man looked quite pail.
4 Behind a fur tree lurked a bear waiting for its prey.
5 He was the life and sole of the party.
6 We looked up and saw an enormous eagle perched on the bow of the tree.
7 It was a beautiful sight for a picnic.
8 He intends to buy some new softwear for his computer.
9 In the end we had to use a chisel to prize open the wooden crate.
10 We had to dress very formerly for the occasion.
11 His only response was to give her a rye smile.
12 It pored with rain and we all got soaked.
13 We were extremely greatful to them for their support.

Now check your answers and then consult the **Reference** section before going on to **B**.

Reference

Words that sound alike but are spelt differently are known as 'homophones'. The term is derived from two Greek words: *homo* (= same) and *phone* (= sound). Some homophones are spelt so differently that they do not usually cause spelling problems once you know the words.

e.g.   you, ewe (female sheep), yew (type of tree)

There are, however, five problem areas that you should be aware of when checking your spelling.

a Be careful not to confuse the <u>possessive</u> form of a word with other forms.

e.g.   <u>its</u> price / <u>it's</u> expensive; <u>their</u> car / up <u>there</u> / <u>they're</u> late; it is <u>theirs</u> / <u>there's</u> no need

b Be careful with words that have silent letters.

e.g.   would, write, whole, knight, whine, answer, sword

c Be particularly alert to pairs of words where just one letter may completely change the meaning.

e.g. canvas (a type of cloth), canvass (seek votes/political support); die/dying (stop living), dye/dyeing (change the colour of things)

d A change of letter may change the grammar of a word.

e.g. practice (noun), practise (verb); licence (noun), license (verb); dependant (noun), dependent (adjective)

e Above all, try not to misspell very basic words.

e.g. break/brake; meet/meat; week/weak; too/two/to; steal/steel; fair/fare

B

Task 1 Use one of the words provided to fill in each gap below.

1 *dependant / dependent*
   She is financially _____ on her parents.
2 *counsellor / councillor*
   A _____ is a politician involved in local government.
3 *hoard / horde*
   The miser kept a _____ of coins hidden under his bed.
4 *wet / whet*
   They served him with an aperitif to _____ his appetite.
5 *write / right / rite / wright*
   William Shakespeare was a play_____ .

Score: /5

Task 2 How many spelling mistakes can you find in the sentences below? Underline and correct each mistake.

1 Fortunately there were some lifeboys on the keyside. We grabbed one and through it into the water.
2 My grandmother taut me how to need doe and bake bred.
3 We were not shore how badly the dog had hurt it's pore, but there was no doubt that it was in grate pane.
4 We had to laugh when Mustapha started flexing his puny mussels on the beech.
5 Their doing there work over they're.
6 We tried to warn him, but he was to far away to here us.
7 Practically the hole nation went into morning when Princess Diana dyed in a car accident.
8 For lunch I had a peace of stake while my brother had place and chips.

Score: /25

Informal speech (vocabulary)

A

Supply an alternative word or phrase for the words that have been underlined.

1. I <u>got</u> <u>loads of</u> presents <u>off</u> my cousins.
2. I asked him where he had <u>nicked</u> all <u>that stuff</u> from.
3. He <u>did</u> me out of £10.
4. It's <u>a good thing</u> we booked our tickets early.
5. I usually have a bath <u>last thing</u> before I go to bed.
6. <u>Say</u> you won the lottery, what would you do?
7. The test was <u>dead</u> easy.
8. She's <u>a bit</u> <u>stuck up</u>.
9. You should <u>stick</u> up for your principles.
10. She told him to <u>stick</u> to the point.
11. He <u>got</u> really <u>mad</u> when I told him he had to <u>get</u> his own dinner for once.
12. He asked us to wait for <u>a bit</u>.

Now check your answers and then consult the **Reference** section before going on to **B**.

Reference

a Informal English (i.e. 'colloquial' English) is the relaxed form of English that we use in speech and in personal letters. It is the sort of English that you may well find in advertisements and popular newspapers. In formal written English, however, you should be careful not to use language that is either too 'familiar' or too loose in meaning. Words like *loads*, *lots*, *stuff*, *crap* and *ain't* should be avoided. Equally, you should try to avoid – or, at least, to keep to a minimum – such overused words as *get* and *bit*.

b Whilst it is important to recognise that a clear distinction exists between spoken and written English, it is equally important not to make one's writing too stiff and formal. For instance, one cannot always avoid *get* in written English, and it is wrong to do so if the result is a stilted phrase or sentence.

Sometimes, too, a colloquial expression can add colour to one's writing. For example, the informal expression *he gave me the creeps* – although not as literary or 'elegant' as *he made my flesh creep* – conveys much more emotion than *he made me feel nervous*, and is slightly less theatrical than *he filled me with horror*.

B

Task 1 Supply an alternative word or phrase for the words in italics.

1 She said she didn't mind *a bit*.
2 It's *a bit* cold in here.
3 He said he had *a bit of a headache*.
4 There was *a bit of an argument*.
5 She's feeling *a bit* better this morning.
6 The boat was smashed *to bits* on the rocks.
7 He has *a fair bit of* money in the bank.
8 He was *thrilled to bits* when he heard the news.
9 Have you got a *bit* of paper I can write on?
10 Be careful. That *bit* of the pond is full of mud.   Score: /10

Task 2 Replace the words in italics with an alternative word or phrase.

1 Eventually he *got* careless and *got* caught by the police.
2 The bullet *got* her in the neck.
3 He *got* me by the arm and tried to pull me across the road.
4 We *got* chatting and discovered we were related.
5 I didn't *get* the joke and asked him to repeat it.
6 I am not sure what this writer is *getting at*.
7 You'll *get nowhere* by shouting at him.
8 At times she *gets a bit carried away*.
9 What *gets* me is her ingratitude.
10 It was *getting on for* midnight when we finally set off.
11 He leaves home so early and *gets back* so late that he hardly ever *gets* to see his children.
12 The heat started to *get to* me, so I asked Michael to *get* me a glass of water.   Score: /15

Task 3 Replace the words in italics with an alternative word or phrase.

1 She *wasn't half cross* when I told her what had happened.
2 She said she would do it, but she *chickened out* at the last moment.
3 The business went *bust*.
4 He *chucked* the ball over the fence.
5 She has decided to *pack in* her present job.
6 He doesn't have a television, *never mind* a video-recorder.
7 They went to *no end* of trouble to help us out.
8 I *reckon* he's *off his head*.
9 He claimed that the shopkeeper had *ripped him off*.   Score: /10

10 Informal speech (grammar) 1

A

| Task |

Correct the sentences below.

1 There's plenty of things that you can do.
2 You should of told me earlier.
3 When he was questioned by the police, he said he hadn't seen nothing.
4 Me and Barry went swimming on Saturday.
5 We went down the park for a game of football.
6 I thought he would find the test very difficult, but he did it real quick and without a single mistake.
7 My mother and I was walking down the road when we heard a loud shriek behind us.
8 If I was you, I would see a doctor.
9 Like I've said before, I don't see why I should help her.
10 Trevor definitely took the money. I seen him do it.

Now check your answers and then consult the **Reference** section before going on to **B**.

Reference

a In spoken English, we tend to use *there's* with both singular and plural words or phrases.

e.g. There's <u>someone</u> to see you. / There's <u>some people</u> to see you.

In written English, we should only use *there's* (= there is) with a singular word or phrase.

e.g. There's <u>a gentleman</u> waiting for you. / There *are* <u>some gentlemen</u> waiting for you.

NB Be careful with *a lot of*: e.g. *There's* <u>a lot of noise</u> outside. / *There are* <u>a lot of people</u> outside.

b The construction *should of* ... does not exist in English grammar. After such verbs as *will, may, might, can, could, should, would* and *ought to*, we always use the infinitive form of a verb.

e.g. He should <u>do</u> it. (present infinitive) / He should <u>have done</u> it. (past infinitive)

When pronounced quickly, *should have done* sounds like *should of done* – and that is why it is such a common mistake to write *of* instead of *have* after these particular verbs.

c Avoid double negatives.

e.g. I know nothing. = I don't know <u>anything</u>. / I saw nobody. = I didn't see <u>anybody</u>. / I have no friends. = I don't have <u>any</u> friends.

d The pronoun *me* is an object pronoun. The pronoun *I* is a subject pronoun.

e.g. She only invited Lorna and me. / Lorna and I went together.

e In written English, you should never use *down* to mean 'to' or 'at'.

e.g. Let's go down the pub. (informal English) / They went to the pub. (written English)

f In written English, make sure that you do not confuse adjectives with adverbs.

e.g. It's a <u>real</u> pity he cannot come. (*real* is an adjective qualifying a noun)
I am <u>really</u> sorry I cannot come. (*really* is an adverb qualifying an adjective)
He is a <u>slow</u> driver. (*slow* is an adjective qualifying a noun)
He drives <u>slowly</u>. (*slowly* is an adverb qualifying a verb)

(See also Unit 17.)

g In written English, always check subject/verb agreement.

e.g. My brother <u>doesn't</u> eat meat. / My father and my brother <u>don't</u> eat meat.

h In written English, you should use *were* instead of *was* after *if*, *if only* and *I wish*.

e.g. If I were you, I wouldn't buy that dress. / If only he were here. / I wish I were younger.

i In spoken English, we often use *like* with a subject and verb.

e.g. "You look like you have seen a ghost." / "He doesn't shout at us, like the other teachers do."

In written English, however, you should use *as* with a clause or prepositional phrase.

e.g. As I have already indicated, we should ... / In this country, as in most countries, we ...

If a clause follows a verb that carries the idea of 'give the impression that' or 'apparently', you should use *as if* or *as though*.

e.g. She looked as if she had seen a ghost.

j In written English, it is important not to confuse the <u>simple past</u> form of an irregular verb (e.g. did, broke, saw) with its <u>past participle</u> (e.g. done, broken, seen).

e.g. I did the work yesterday. / The work was done yesterday. / I have done the work.

(See also Unit 22.)

B

Correct any mistakes in the sentences below. Tick any sentence that is grammatically correct.

1 He looked like he needed a holiday.

2 She looked like an angel.

3 She looked like she had been crying.

4 She acted like she owned the place.

5 We went to Brighton, like we do every year.

6 If I had been in his position, I would of done exactly what he done.

7 You might of told me you had invited an extra twenty people to the party!

8 They searched the whole house, but they didn't find nothing incriminating.

9 He said that he hardly never went out in the evenings.

10 The teacher said that she did not want to hear no more noise.

11 They were sitting quite happy in the car.

12 He said he was quite happy to wait in the car.

13 He looked anxious at his watch.

14 There's usually a lot more accidents on the motorways when it is foggy.

15 If I was the headteacher of this school, I would abolish homework.

16 My sister works down the local supermarket.

17 My brother and I was putting up our tent when a sudden gust of wind blew it away.

18 Everybody in the class were interested when I suggested an end-of-term party.

19 He don't know what he's talking about.

20 As he begun to speak, the doorbell rang.

Score: /20

11 Informal speech (grammar) 2

A

| Task |

Below you will find some typical grammatical mistakes made in spoken English. Correct each mistake.

1 It's not the cost what worries me, it's the time it will take.
2 It was the way he dealt with the problem what impressed us most.
3 The people what live in the cottage opposite us are not very friendly.
4 "My daughter's happiness is all what matters," he said.
5 "I need to buy a birthday card," she said.
   "For who?" he asked.
6 He is someone in who I have complete faith.
7 It's no use me telling him. He never listens to me.
8 Excuse me asking, but are you wearing a wig?
9 He said he would show me a more quicker way of doing it.
10 Less than a hundred people attended the concert.
11 No sooner had I watered the plants in the garden then it began to rain.
12 I have never and would never do such a thing!

Now check your answers and then consult the **Reference** section before going on to **B**.

Reference

a You should never use *what* as a substitute for *that*, *which* or *who*. This confusion often arises because one of the functions of *what* is to act as a substitute for *the thing that* or *the things that*.

e.g. The thing that surprised me was how long it took. = What surprised me was how long it took.

b Whether we use *who* or *whom* depends on word order. Following a preposition, *who* becomes *whom*.

e.g. Who were you referring to? = To whom were you referring? (more formal English)

c Occasionally, you may need to convert an object pronoun (e.g. me, you, him) into a possessive pronoun (e.g. my, your, his) in front of a gerund. (A gerund is a verbal noun ending in *-ing*.) We do this to show that, rather than functioning in its own right, the pronoun is actually part of a noun phrase.

e.g. I don't like <u>him</u>. / I don't like <u>his</u> interrupting me like that.

'I don't like <u>him</u>' means 'I don't like him as a person'.
'I don't like <u>his interrupting me like that</u>' means 'I don't like <u>his</u> <u>interruptions</u>'. In this case, *interrupting* is not a verb but a verbal noun (or gerund): it looks like a verb, but is used like a noun.

d Do not give an adjective a double comparative form. Either an adjective will end in *-er* (e.g. bigger, smaller, brighter) or it will be preceded by *more* (e.g. more interesting, more intelligent).

e *fewer / less*

- Before a plural noun, you should use *fewer* rather than *less*.

e.g. fewer jobs, fewer people, fewer students

- Use *fewer than* before a number of people or things.

e.g. fewer than twenty students

- use *less than* before an amount or measurement.

e.g. less than twenty pounds a week / less than a hundred miles

f Note the following pattern: <u>No sooner</u> had I turned my back <u>than</u> they started making a noise again.

g Always complete the first of two different verb forms – even if it means repeating the verb.

e.g. I have never <u>spoken</u> and would never <u>speak</u> to her in such a way.

B

| Task |

Correct any sentence that contains a grammatical mistake. Tick any sentence that is grammatically correct.

1 My mother doesn't like the idea of me travelling abroad on my own.
2 The only thing what I don't like about her is that she can be a bit bossy at times.
3 He is not prepared to work for less than three hundred pounds a week.
4 You won't meet a more nicer person than Daksha.
5 No sooner had she entered the room then everyone started clapping and cheering.
6 On the front of the envelope was written: 'To whom it may concern'.
7 Everything what she said was absolutely true, and I told her so.
8 There have been less accidents on this stretch of the motorway since the introduction of speed traps.

9   To who shall I address this letter?

10 I am afraid that there is very little possibility of him passing the exam.

11 The police wanted to know from who we had obtained the information.

12 It was her rudeness that shocked us.

13 She objected to me smoking in her house.

14 It was the discovery of an enormous hole over the South Pole what made people aware of the damage being done to the ozone layer.

15 He's been making less spelling mistakes since he started attending Mr Brown's class.

16 "Those are not the shoes what I ordered," he said.

17 To who does this belong?

18 They didn't offer him the job, despite him being a competent carpenter and joiner.

19 I was delighted with the present: it was exactly what I wanted.

20 I have always and will always follow my instincts in such matters.

Score: /20

12 Nouns ending in *-er, -or, -ar*

A

Task

Complete each word with one of the following suffixes: *-er, -or, -ar*.

1 a translat__ 2 a smuggl__ 3 gramm__ 4 a trait__ 5 a solicit__
6 a lawy__ 7 a radiat__ 8 an announc__ 9 a spectat__
10 a caterpill__ 11 a li__ 12 a doct__ 13 a sail__ 14 a coll__
15 a dictat__ 16 a prison__ 17 a visit__ 18 a word-process__
19 an auth__ 20 a burgl__

Now check your answers and then consult the **Reference** section before going on to **B**.

Reference

a The suffixes *-er, -or* and *-ar* are often misspelt because they usually sound the same. As you read the rules of thumb below, bear in mind that the commonest suffix of the three is *-er*.

b Nouns that end in *-er* and *-or* are known as 'agent' nouns because, generally speaking, they show the specific job, occupation or function of a person or thing.

e.g. a *singer* is someone who sings (for a living); a *translator* is somebody who translates; a *duplicator* is a machine that duplicates things

c An 'agent' noun may also show the specific activity that someone is involved in.

e.g. a *smuggler* is someone involved in smuggling goods; a *visitor* is someone who is paying a visit; a *competitor* is someone involved in a competition

d A technical word of Latin origin is more likely to end in *-or*.

e.g. calculator, incubator, duplicator, processor, monitor, transistor, projector

Note, however, the following: printer, computer, photocopier, stapler, typewriter, container.

e When referring to a person's trade or occupation, *-er* is more common than *-or*.

e.g. *-er*: boxer, carpenter, fighter, hunter, interpreter, painter, teacher, writer
-or: decorator, sailor, tailor

f On the other hand, formal positions or people's titles are often – but not always – denoted by *-or*.

e.g.   ambassador, author, chancellor, conqueror, councillor, counsellor, emperor, professor, proprietor, rector, senator, solicitor, sponsor, successor, suitor, surveyor

g Occasionally an agent word may be spelt with either -er or -or. In such cases, -er denotes a person.

e.g.   a *resister* is someone who resists; a *resistor* is an electrical device

NB Do not confuse a *miner* (someone who works in a mine) with a *minor* (a young person not yet legally an adult).

h -ar is found at the end of just a few agent nouns. The main ones are: beggar, burglar, liar, scholar.

i Other common nouns ending in -ar include: altar, calendar, caterpillar, cellar, collar, dollar, grammar, guitar, hangar, mortar, nectar, pillar, sugar, vicar, vinegar.

NB Be careful not to confuse the following words: an *altar* (noun) is found in a church / to *alter* (verb) = to change; a *hangar* is where one keeps aircraft / a *hanger* is used for hanging up clothes.

B

| Task 1 | Complete each word with one of the following suffixes: -er, -or, -ar. |

1 a surviv__   2 a begg__   3 an inspect__   4 vineg__   5 an edit__
6 a garden__   7 a govern__   8 a ventilat__   9 a comput__
10 a thermomet__   Score: /10

| Task 2 | Where a word is incomplete, add one of the following suffixes: -er, -or, -ar. |

1 William the Conquer__ invaded England in 1066.
2 The direct__ of a play or film has the same task as the conduct__ of an orchestra. He or she rehearses the act__s and helps them to interpret their parts.
3 The transist__ radio was invented in 1948.
4 When Gustave Eiffel designed his famous Eiffel Tower in Paris, object__s said it would be a danger to birds.
5 The first steam engine was built in 1805 by the English invent__ Richard Trevithick.
6 James Cook (1728–79) was an English explor__ and navigat__ .
7 By about 2800 BC the Egyptians had invented a calend__ to keep track of time.
8 The Roman Emper__ Nero was the only competit__ to be awarded first place in an Olympic competition without winning or even finishing the race.   Score: /12

13 Nouns ending in *-ence, -ance*

A

| Task | Where a word is incomplete, insert either *-ence* or *-ance*.

1 They were impressed by his eloqu_____ .
2 They did not appreciate the import_____ of the discovery.
3 Appear_____s can be deceptive.
4 Finish it off at your conveni_____ .
5 His secretary deals with all the correspond_____ .
6 The two countries formed an alli_____ .
7 She thanked him for his assist_____ .
8 What a coincid_____ !
9 He protested his innoc_____ .
10 It was a senseless act of viol_____ .
11 He was a member of the French Resist_____ during the war.
12 They are fighting for independ_____ .
13 What I have to tell you is in strict confid_____ .
14 A Hoover is an example of a domestic appli_____ .
15 The judge questioned the relev_____ of the evid_____ that was being given.

Now check your answers and then consult the **Reference** section before going on to **B**.

Reference

The suffixes *-ence* and *-ance* are used to form abstract nouns. There is no easy way of distinguishing between these two suffixes, but there are certain guidelines that are worth bearing in mind.

a *-ence* follows a soft *c* or *g*.

e.g.   innocence, adolescence, intelligence

-ance follows a hard *c* or *g*.

e.g.   significance, elegance, arrogance
Exceptions: allegiance, vengeance

b A noun will usually end in *-ence* rather than *-ance* if the root verb connected with it ends in *-ere*.

e.g.   interfere - interference; cohere - coherence; revere - reverence
Exception: persevere - perseverance

c A noun will usually end in *-ance* rather than *-ence* if the verb connected with it ends in *-ear*, *-ure* or *-y*.

e.g. appear - appearance; assure - assurance; insure - insurance; rely - reliance; ally - alliance; defy - defiance

NB If a root verb ends in a consonant + *-y*, the *y* will change to *i* before *-ance*.

d Many words follow a logical pattern.

e.g. independ<u>ent</u> - independ<u>ence</u>; confid<u>ent</u> - confid<u>ence</u>; relev<u>ant</u> - relev<u>ance</u>; attend<u>ant</u> - attend<u>ance</u>

e Note carefully the spelling of each of the following verbs and nouns:

e.g. maintain - maintenance; remember - remembrance; hinder - hindrance; excel - excellence; admit - admittance

B

| Task 1 | Complete each sentence by forming an appropriate noun from the verb given in brackets.

1 His sudden _____ mystified the whole village. (disappear)
2 She needed a lot of _____ before she would continue. (reassure)
3 He proved to be more of a _____ than a help. (hinder)
4 A special memorial service was held on _____ Sunday. (remember)
5 The house was very old and needed a lot of _____ . (maintain)
6 The notice said, 'Private – no _____'. (admit)
7 The school he attends is noted for its academic _____ . (excel)   Score: 7

| Task 2 | Where a word is incomplete, insert either *-ence* or *-ance*.

1 Abs_____ makes the heart grow fonder.
2 'If a man does not make new aquaint_____ as he advances through life, he will soon find himself alone.' (Samuel Johnson)
3 'But with the morning, cool repent_____ came.' (Sir Walter Scott)
4 'Had we lived, I should have had a tale to tell of the hardihood, endur_____ and courage of my companions which would have stirred the heart of every Englishman. These rough notes and our dead bodies must tell the tale.' (Robert Falcon Scott)

5 'Beware that you do not lose the subst_____ by grasping at the shadow.' (Aesop)

6 'Sil_____ is the virtue of fools.' (Francis Bacon)

7 'A sufficient and sure method of civilisation is the influ_____ of good women.' (Emerson)

8 'It is ridiculous for any man to criticise the works of another if he has not distinguished himself by his own perform_____s.' (Addison)

9 'Knowledge is the child of experi_____ .' (Leonardo da Vinci)

10 'The differ_____ between journalism and literature is that journalism is unreadable and literature is never read.' (Oscar Wilde)

11 Leonard Bacon, a famous nineteenth-century American theologian, was once addressing a religious confer_____ when he said something that annoyed a member of the audi_____ .
"Why, I never heard of such a thing in all my life!" shouted the outraged man.
"I'm terribly sorry," said Bacon, "but I cannot allow your ignor_____ , however vast, to prejudice my knowledge, however small."

Score: /13

Words ending in *-ary, -ery, -ory, -ury*

A

Where a word is incomplete, add one of the following endings: *-ary, -ery, -ory, -ury*.

1 There was an explosion in the laborat____ .
2 The torch needs a new batt____ .
3 She needs to learn more vocabul____ .
4 He was awarded a medal for brav____ .
5 It wasn't a serious inj____ .
6 Water is necess____ for life.
7 Her work is unsatisfact____ .
8 Would you spend a night alone in a cemet____ ?
9 She spends most weekends doing volunt____ work.
10 The car skidded on the slipp____ road.
11 The soldier was arrested by the milit____ police.
12 Most of the machin____ in the fact____ is obsolete.
13 I couldn't find his number in the telephone direct____ .
14 Tom's brother is a mission____ in Africa.
15 The envelopes are kept in the station____ cupboard.

Now check your answers and then consult the **Reference** section before going on to **B**.

Reference

There are no hard and fast rules to help you decide whether a word should end in *-ary, -ery, -ory* or *-ury*. There are, however, a few rules of thumb that are worth bearing in mind.

a It's often possible to work out the spelling of a word by thinking of a word related to it.

e.g. burglar - burglary; robber - robbery; director - directory; injure - injury

b Words ending in *-ery* are usually nouns.

e.g. cemetery, stationery, machinery
Main exceptions: slippery, fiery, watery

c Nouns ending in *-ery* often contain a complete smaller word within them.

e.g. (deliver)y; (scene)ry; (green)ery; (adult)ery

d Very few words end in *-ury*, and they are usually nouns.

e.g. century, fury, injury, jury, mercury, perjury, treasury
Exception: bury

e Words ending in *-ary* and *-ory* may be adjectives or nouns.

e.g. Adjectives (*-ary*): customary, necessary, stationary (= not moving),
voluntary
Nouns (*-ary*): anniversary, dictionary, library, salary
Adjectives (*-ory*): advisory, compulsory, extrasensory, obligatory
Nouns (*-ory*): category, dormitory, factory, history, memory

B

Task

Where a word is incomplete, add one of the following endings: *-ary*, *-ery*,
-ory, *-ury*.

1 Every student should have a diction_____ .
2 Where is the nearest libr_____ ?
3 He is here in an advis_____ capacity only.
4 The general word for sweets of all kinds is 'confection_____'.
5 He has fond memories of his prim_____ school.
6 His birthday is in Febru_____ .
7 Is he looking for a tempor_____ or a permanent position?
8 It is compuls_____ to study English at school.
9 The students had to write a summ_____ of what they had read.
10 An itiner_____ is a detailed plan of a journey.
11 He was sent to prison for committing perj_____ .
12 She is suffering from loss of mem_____ .
13 What an extraordin_____ thing to say!
14 He predicted a landslide vict_____ for the Conservatives.
15 Tomorrow is their wedding annivers_____ .
16 She used to work as a secret_____ .
17 He leads a solit_____ existence.
18 The lion is a predat_____ beast.
19 The scen_____ in Switzerland is magnificent.
20 In some countries you can be imprisoned for adult_____ .
21 A tribut_____ is a river or stream which discharges its waters
into a larger river or stream.
22 An estu_____ is the broad mouth of a river when it widens out
before reaching the sea.
23 I am not bored. On the contr_____ , I think this is fascinating.
24 He comes from Hung_____ .
25 Haemophilia is a heredit_____ disease.
26 An animal will always defend its territ_____ .
27 He asked if he could use the lavat_____ .

Score: /27

15 Words ending in *-us, -ous, -ious, -eous*

A

| Task |

Where a word is incomplete, add *-us, -ous, -ious* or *-eous*.

1 We are anx____ to find out the truth.
2 He was attacked by a feroc____ dog.
3 That was very gener____ of him.
4 Her son is very ambit____ .
5 What a ludicr____ thing to say!
6 I have never met a more court____ person than John.
7 She felt quite self-consc____ .
8 He is a notor____ criminal.
9 What a pomp____ fool he is!
10 He joined a relig____ sect when he was sixteen.
11 The meal was delic____ .
12 Your daughter has a vir____ and should stay in bed.
13 What they propose is outrag____ !
14 His spelling is atroc____ .
15 It was a spontan____ decision.

Now check your answers and then consult the **Reference** section before going on to **B**.

Reference

a Words that end in *-us* tend to be <u>nouns</u> of Latin origin.

e.g. cactus, fungus, nucleus, opus, radius, stimulus, terminus

Words that end in *-ous, -ious* and *-eous* tend to be <u>adjectives</u>.

b To avoid confusing *-eous* and *-ious*, it is best to learn by heart the most common adjectives ending in *-eous*.

e.g. advantageous, courageous, courteous, erroneous, gorgeous, hideous, instantaneous, miscellaneous, nauseous, outrageous, simultaneous, spontaneous

You should also be aware of the most common adjectives that end in *-ious*, but where the *i* sounds like *e*.

e.g. curious, delirious, hilarious, laborious, notorious, previous, serious

c To avoid confusing *-ous* and *-ious*, you should note that the letters *t, c* and *x* combine with *-ious* to give us a *sh* sound.

e.g. ambitious, anxious, conscientious, conscious, delicious, ferocious, luscious, obnoxious, pretentious, spacious, superstitious

d Note the stem changes when *-ous* is added to the following words:
- grief - grievous; mischief - mischievous
- humour - humorous; rigour - rigorous; vigour - vigorous
- disaster - disastrous; monster - monstrous

e Note that an *-ious* ending may be the result of a *y* changing to *i* when *-ous* is added.

e.g.   envy - envious; fury - furious; mystery - mysterious; vary - various

f Sometimes *u* is placed before *-ous*.

e.g.   ambiguous, conspicuous, promiscuous

g In most other cases when deciding between *-ous* and *-ious*, the sound of the word should indicate whether an *i* is necessary.

e.g.   adventurous, pompous, tedious

B

Task 1   Form an appropriate adjective from the word in brackets.

1 He can be quite _____ at times. (humour)
2 It was a _____ crime. (monster)
3 The film was _____ . (hilarity)
4 She was very upset by the _____ gossip. (malice)
5 Children are often _____ . (mischief)
6 He'll be _____ when he finds out. (fury)
7 The _____ stranger did not say a word. (mystery)
8 Some _____ exercise will do you good. (vigour)
9 It was a _____ decision. (courage)
10 The flat is quite _____ . (space)   Score: /10

Task 2   Where a word is incomplete, add *-us*, *-ous*, *-ious* or *-eous*.

1 All the characters portrayed in this novel are fictit____ .
2 Is that disease contag____ ?
3 He appeared obliv____ to his surroundings.
4 He said he had never eaten octop____ before.
5 He was the victim of a particularly vic____ attack.
6 Who's that suspic____ -looking man?
7 What a hid____ shirt!
8 How can you afford to rent such a luxur____ flat?
9 He admitted that he had been wrong the prev____ time.
10 The effect was instantan____ .
11 He tried to impress us, but we found him rather pretent____ .
12 She was a shy but conscient____ student.   Score: /12

16 Some awkward nouns and adjectives

A

Task 1 Complete each sentence by forming an appropriate adjective or noun from the word given in brackets.

1 Twenty plus twenty equals _____ . (four)
2 He came _____ in the race. (nine)
3 December is the _____ month of the year. (twelve)
4 We demanded an immediate _____ . (explain)
5 One should avoid the _____ mark in formal writing. (exclaim)
6 To see our teacher dancing the tango so passionately was quite a _____ . (reveal)
7 If there is any _____ of that kind of behaviour, I shall send you out of the room. (repeat)
8 Suddenly the aeroplane started losing _____ . (high)

Task 2 Correct any spelling mistakes in the sentences below.

1 We were suprised to find how knowledgable he was.
2 At the beggining of the course he wasn't very co-operative, but by the end there was a noticable difference in his attitude.
3 We were looking forward to an exiting match, but our team's performance was very dissapointing.
4 He said that desparate measures were needed to save the enviroment.
5 What he did wasn't just iresponsible, it was absolutely unforgiveable.

Now check your answers and then consult the **Reference** section before going on to **B**.

Reference

To help you improve your spelling, make sure that you are aware of the following problem areas:

a Certain numbers cause more spelling problems than others.

e.g.   eight, eighth, ninth, twelfth, twentieth, forty, eighty, ninety-nine

b With a particular group of verbs, the verb drops a vowel when it is turned into a noun.

e.g.   enter - entrance; exclaim - exclamation; explain - explanation;

proclaim - proclamation; pronounce - pronunciation; repeat - repetition; reveal - revelation

c Note carefully the letters that have been underlined in the following words: desperate, separate, surprised, excited, height, government, environment.

d When *-ible* or *-able* is added to a root word ending in *-e*, the *e* is usually dropped except after a soft *c* or *g*.

e.g.   sensible, believable, forgivable   <u>but</u>   noticeable, knowledgeable

e Note the double consonants in the following words: begi<u>nn</u>ing, cance<u>ll</u>ation, insta<u>ll</u>ation, forge<u>tt</u>able.

f Be careful when adding a negative prefix to a word.

e.g.   *dis-* + appointed = disappointed; *dis-* + satisfied = dissatisfied; *ir-* + responsible = irresponsible; *il-* + legal = illegal

B

Task 1

Complete each sentence with a suitable <u>negative</u> adjective formed from the word given in brackets. Each adjective needs to start with an appropriate negative prefix (e.g. *in-*, *un-*, *ir-*) and will end in *-able*.

1 Unfortunately he is suffering from an _____ disease. (cure)
2 Their differences are _____ . (reconcile)
3 It was an _____ experience. (forget)
4 I knew it was him. His voice is _____ . (mistake)
5 The pain was _____ . (describe)
6 This priceless vase is _____ . (replace)
7 The truth must be faced – however _____ it may be. (palate)   Score: /7

Task 2

Correct any spelling mistakes in the sentences below.

1 Following their proclaimation of independence, the rebels have declared war on the present goverment.
2 The students come in through a seperate enterance.
3 His pronounciation is excellent.
4 What you have just said is both irational and irelevant.
5 There was a note of dissaproval in his voice.
6 His arguments are ilogical and his handwriting is ilegible.
7 He gets the answer right ninty-nine times out of a hundred.
8 All trains were subject to delay and cancelation.
9 Although her story sounded plausible, I was disatisfied with some of the answers she gave.
10 He said he hated everything about the twentyeth century and wished he had been born in the eighteenth century.   Score: /14

17 Forming and using adverbs

A

Task 1

How many spelling mistakes can you find in the sentences below? Tick any sentence that does not contain a spelling mistake.

1   He accidently set fire to her dress.
2   The Romans were so fond of eating mice that the upper classes raised them domesticly. The rodents were kept in specialy designed cages and were fed a mixture of nuts.
3   Monkeys' heads have been successfully transplanted at Case Western Reserve University in Cleveland, Ohio.
4   As far as we know, they are happyly married.
5   He drove so recklessley that we feared for our lives.
6   She is incredibley lucky to be alive.
7   She's just had a nasty shock, so treat her gentley.
8   We can't possibley help her.
9   The door opens automatically.
10   He whistled cheerfuly.

Task 2

Is there any difference in meaning between the two sentences below?

a His hair badly needs cutting. *b* His hair needs cutting badly.

Task 3

Look at the following two sentences and then answer the questions below:

a "I don't particularly want to go there," she said.
b "I particularly don't want to go there," she said.

Which is the stronger statement of the two? In which sentence is the speaker merely expressing some reluctance?

Task 4

Look at the two sentences below. Which one contains a 'split infinitive'?

a He asked me to note down carefully everything that was said at the meeting.
b He asked me to carefully note down everything that was said at the meeting.

Now check your answers and then consult the **Reference** section before going on to **B**.

Reference

a An adverb modifies a verb, an adjective or another adverb. Many adverbs end in -*ly*, and they are formed in the following way:
- An adverb ending in -*ly* is formed from an adjective.
- For most words, take the full form of the adjective and simply add -*ly*. If the adjective already ends in an -*l*, you will end up with -*lly*.

e.g. real - really; careful - carefully

- The final -*e* of an adjective is not usually dropped.

e.g. rare - rarely; bare - barely

Exceptions (1): true - truly; due - duly; whole - wholly
(2): If an adjective ends in -*le*, drop the *e* and add only -*y*.

e.g. reasonable - reasonably; terrible - terribly; idle -idly

- If an adjective ends in a consonant + -*y*, drop the *y* and add -*ily*.

e.g. steady - steadily; merry - merrily; temporary - temporarily; easy - easily

Exceptions: shy - shyly; sly - slyly; dry - dryly/drily

- After -*ic*, the ending is usually -*ally*.

e.g. basic - basically

Exception: publicly

b Where you position an adverb will be determined by the rhythm of the sentence and the meaning intended. As a general rule, do not separate a verb from its object.

e.g. He speaks French and Spanish fluently. / He fully understands the consequences of his actions.

c A 'split infinitive' occurs when a word (usually an adverb) comes between *to* and a verb.

e.g. to really believe, to boldly go, to clearly see

The idea of the split infinitive being grammatically incorrect originated in the nineteenth century when certain grammarians insisted on modelling the English language on Latin grammar (which does not allow for a 'split infinitive' because the Latin infinitive is a single word). Nowadays, however, most grammarians agree that it is perfectly acceptable to split an infinitive if there are good reasons for doing so. The main rule when positioning adverbs is that the sentence should sound natural and be clear in meaning.

B

Using the underlined words as the basis for your answer, rephrase each sentence below without changing its meaning. Each sentence should contain an adverb. Start your sentence as indicated in brackets.

> e.g. He was <u>foolish</u> enough <u>to believe</u> everything he read in the papers. (He ...)
> = He foolishly believed everything he read in the papers.

1 His <u>response</u> to her request was <u>sympathetic</u>. (He ...)
2 They have the <u>occasional argument</u>, like all couples. (They ...)
3 He demanded their <u>unconditional surrender</u>. (He said that they had to ...)
4 Her <u>behaviour</u> was <u>unpredictable</u>. (She ...)
5 My <u>original plan</u> was to have a very quiet wedding. (I had ...)
6 His proposal came in for <u>heavy criticism</u> from everybody concerned. (His proposal was ...)
7 Their <u>struggle</u> against impossible odds was <u>heroic</u>. (They ...)
8 His <u>injuries</u> were <u>fatal</u>. (He was ...)
9 The <u>probable cause</u> of the fire was an electrical fault. (The fire was ...)
10 Her <u>death</u> was <u>peaceful</u>. (She ...)

11 There has been a <u>dramatic rise</u> in the cost of petrol. (The cost of petrol has ...)
12 The <u>suffering</u> they endured was <u>terrible</u>. (They ...)
13 It was very <u>sensible</u> of her <u>to call</u> the police. (She ...)
14 He gave her an <u>angry look</u>. (He ...)
15 Despite his <u>profuse apologies</u>, she would not forgive him. (Although he ...)

Score: /15

43

Confusing words 3

A

Choose the correct alternative in brackets.

1 She has a (flair / flare) for languages.
2 Rheumatism (inflicts / afflicts) both the young and the old.
3 Be careful how you (broach / brooch) the subject with him.
4 My best friend has decided to leave Ireland and (emigrate / immigrate) to Australia.
5 We waited for the results with (baited / bated) breath.
6 If he persists in (flouting / flaunting) all our rules and regulations, we shall have to exclude him from school.
7 Make sure you lock the (filing / filling) cabinet.
8 I am sure that I will see her (some time / sometime) this week.
9 He said that he had done his homework but had (forgotten / left) his book at home.
10 The hotel was surrounded by (luxurious / luxuriant) tropical vegetation.
11 They discovered that she was a (heroin / heroine) addict.

Now check your answers and then consult the **Reference** section before going on to **B**.

Reference

Note carefully the following:

1 flair = natural ability/talent; flare: (a) bright light or flame, (b) a device that produces bright light or coloured smoke.
2 to afflict means to cause someone physical or mental suffering. Something afflicts you or you are afflicted with something. to inflict something on someone means to make someone suffer/experience something unpleasant; to impose something unpleasant on someone.
3 to broach a subject means to raise a matter / bring up a point for discussion; a brooch is an ornament worn on clothes.
4 to emigrate means to go and live in another country; to immigrate means to come into a country in order to live there.
5 with bated breath = anxiously or excitedly; baited is the past form of to bait. (a) to bait a person/animal means to harass/pester/annoy/tease the person or animal intentionally. (b) to bait a hook with a worm means to place a worm on a hook in order to catch a fish.

6 to flout is deliberately to disobey (someone or something) in an open and defiant manner; to flaunt is to exhibit something in such a way that everybody is forced to take notice of it.

7 filing is related to *file*; filling is related to *fill*.

8 some time = a little time / an amount of time; sometime: (a) at some point in time, (b) formerly.

9 to leave = to forget (when we indicate location). Note the different patterns: 'to forget something'; 'to leave something somewhere'.

10 luxurious is related to luxury (expensive/opulent/extremely comfortable); luxuriant is related to healthy growth (thick, lush).

11 heroin is an addictive drug; heroine is the female equivalent of *hero*.

B

| Task |

Choose the correct alternative in brackets.

1 The air strike (afflicted / inflicted) heavy casualties on the enemy troops.

2 I need (some time / sometime) to think about it. I will give you my answer (some time / sometime) next week.

3 She spent half an hour (filing / filling) her nails.

4 A (flare / flair) is often used as a distress signal at sea.

5 "I've (forgotten / left) the tickets," he murmured as they entered the theatre. "I've (forgotten / left) them in the hotel room."

6 She was wearing a very pretty (broach / brooch).

7 The trouble with him is that he likes to (flaunt / flout) his wealth.

8 All her teachers say that she has a (flair / flare) for Maths.

9 They (baited / bated) the trap with a live goat and waited for the tiger to appear.

10 Charlie Watkins, (some time / sometime) soldier of fortune and ex-security guard, was found murdered in his flat last night.

11 I wish he would keep his views to himself and not (afflict / inflict) them on us at every possible opportunity.

12 They stayed in a (luxurious / luxuriant) hotel.

13 What's the name of the actress who plays the (heroin / heroine) in the film?

14 In medieval times, bear-(baiting / bating) was a popular form of entertainment.

15 She is (afflicted / inflicted) with arthritis and can barely walk.

16 "If you continue to (flaunt / flout) the law," warned the judge, "I'll have no alternative but to send you to prison."

Score: /18

19   Confusing words 4

A

Task 1 Choose the correct alternative in brackets.

1 His manner was so (authoritative / authoritarian) that we were too scared to ask any questions.
2 Capital punishment is a highly (emotive / emotional) issue.
3 It is every academic's dream to write the (definite / definitive) book on his or her subject.
4 Comparisons are (odious / odorous).
5 He collects (erotic / exotic) plants, and displays them in his conservatory.
6 That was a (contemptible / contemptuous) thing to do! You should be ashamed of yourself.
7 The families of the (diseased / deceased) are demanding an official inquiry into the circumstances surrounding the sinking of the ship.
8 She still hasn't found an (effective / efficient) remedy for her migraines.
9 Junk food is usually (defective / deficient) in vitamins and vital minerals.
10 He finds (urban / urbane) life too stressful and is hoping to move to the country.
11 Her current boyfriend is a (blond / blonde) Norwegian who speaks impeccable English.
12 We were (quite / quiet) happy to have just a banana for (desert / dessert).

Task 2 Answer the following questions:

1 In one word, what is the opposite of *flammable*?
2 Is a set of separate stories featuring the same characters on television or radio called a *series* or a *serial*?
3 If you are taken by surprise, are you caught *unaware* or *unawares*?

Now check your answers and then consult the **Reference** section before going on to **B**.

Reference

Note carefully the following:

1 <u>authoritative</u>: commanding respect; <u>authoritarian</u>: demanding obedience
2 <u>emotive</u>: arousing strong emotions; <u>emotional</u>: showing emotion / centred on emotion
3 <u>definite</u> = clear, certain, fixed; <u>definitive</u>: (a) not likely to be improved upon, (b) final / best / most authoritative
4 <u>odious</u> = disgusting, hateful; <u>odorous</u>: related to odour (smell)
5 <u>erotic</u>: relating to / arousing sexual desire; <u>exotic</u>: related to tropical countries / unusual and exciting
6 <u>contemptible</u>: deserving contempt; <u>contemptuous</u>: showing contempt
7 <u>deceased</u> = (recently) dead; <u>diseased</u> = infected
8 <u>efficient</u>: working/operating properly and in an organised way; <u>effective</u>: achieving/producing the desired effect
9 <u>deficient</u>: lacking something / not as good as it should be; <u>defective</u>: (a) having a defect or defects, (b) imperfect/incomplete
10 <u>urban</u>: related to city/town; <u>urbane</u> = civilised/confident/refined/well-mannered
11 <u>blond</u>: fair (masculine); <u>blonde</u>: fair (feminine). When describing hair, either *blond* or *blonde* can be used for either gender.
12 <u>quite</u> = fairly, rather; <u>quiet</u> = not noisy
13 <u>a desert</u>: a waterless and treeless region; <u>to desert</u> = to abandon; <u>dessert</u> = pudding/sweet
14 Strangely enough, <u>flammable</u> and <u>inflammable</u> have the same meaning ('can catch fire'). The opposite is <u>non-flammable</u>.
15 <u>a serial</u>: a single story presented in separate instalments; <u>a series</u>: a set of different stories with the same characters
16 <u>unaware</u> = ignorant of / not conscious of; <u>unawares</u> = by surprise

B

| Task |

Choose the correct alternative in brackets.

1 He is a highly (emotional / emotive) person and has been known to burst into tears while making a speech.
2 Under an (authoritarian / authoritative) regime, people do not have the freedom to act as they wish.
3 His behaviour was so (contemptible / contemptuous) that everybody gave him the cold shoulder.
4 The surgeon explained that he would have to remove the (deceased / diseased) kidney.
5 People will not stop using their cars until we have a more (efficient / effective) public transport system.

6 He was a bit too smooth for my liking. I was not impressed by his (urban / urbane) charm and wit.

7 The inspector said that the machinery was (defective / deficient) and needed replacing.

8 As we were crossing the (desert / dessert), a sand storm caught us (unaware / unawares).

9 You should not light a match near (inflammable / non-flammable) material.

10 Professor Thomson's book – considered by many to be the (definite / definitive) work on the subject – gives an (authoritarian / authoritative) account of events leading up to the Spanish Civil War.

11 Legalised abortion is an (emotional / emotive) issue.

12 It was an (odious / odorous) crime and he deserves to be imprisoned for life.

13 He defended the film by claiming that it was (erotic / exotic) rather than pornographic.

14 He replied in such a (contemptible / contemptuous) tone that she took offence and stormed out of the office.

15 Friends and relatives of the (deceased / diseased) attended a special memorial service.

Score: /17

20 Prepositions

A

Task 1 Correct any mistakes in the sentences below.

1 Please keep this to yourself. This is strictly between you and I.
2 The new committee will comprise of ten members: seven students and three teachers.
3 For me, the beauty of this poem consists of its unusual imagery.
4 Glass is made of sand.
5 The criminal's plan was to substitute fake diamonds with the ones he intended to steal.
6 You have got away with it so far, but they will catch you at the end.

Task 2 Fill in each gap with a suitable preposition.

1 He would not agree _____ their demands and asked them to leave the office.
2 This is certainly an improvement _____ your last piece of work.
3 I am surprised _____ you. Of all people, you should have known better.
4 She was robbed _____ her jewellery.
5 They went to South America in search _____ gold.
6 I am fed up _____ being criticised all the time.
7 She says she is acting _____ principle, but I suspect an ulterior motive.
8 Our customs are different _____ yours.
9 When we say that 'life is like a battle', we are comparing life _____ a battle.

Now check your answers and then consult the **Reference** section before going on to **B**.

Reference

a Prepositions are such words as *in*, *of*, *to*, *at*, *from*, *between* and *with*.

b After a preposition, the correct pronoun to use is an object pronoun (i.e. *me*, *you*, *him*, *her*, *it*, *us*, *them*). In the same way that we say *between him and her* (not *between he and she*), so we say *between you and me* (not *between you and I*).

c The committee <u>consists of</u> six members. = The committee <u>is composed of</u> six members. = The committee <u>comprises</u> six members. (no preposition after *comprise*)

d When talking about the main feature/element of something, we use <u>in</u> after *consist*.

e.g. His work <u>consists in</u> helping refugees.

e 'The bottle is <u>made of</u> glass' means that glass has been used to make the bottle (and we can still see the glass). 'Glass is <u>made from</u> sand' means that sand is used to make glass (and, once this happens, the sand can never be sand again).

f Note the following patterns:
He <u>replaced</u> the faulty light-bulb <u>with</u> a new one.
He <u>substituted</u> a new light-bulb <u>for</u> the faulty one.

g <u>in the end</u> = eventually; <u>at the end</u> (of a road/film/book) indicates 'where'

h to agree <u>with</u> something = to approve of something (e.g. an idea); to agree <u>to</u> something = to say yes to / to assent to something (e.g. a proposal)

i We use <u>on</u> with *improvement* when we are making a comparison.

e.g. Model B is a distinct improvement on Model A. (i.e. Model B is much better than Model A.)

j When *surprised* is clearly being used as an adjective, use <u>at</u> rather than <u>by</u>.

e.g. I am surprised at him. (i.e. I find his attitude/behaviour surprising.)

When *surprised* can be seen either as an adjective or as part of a passive construction, use either <u>at</u> or <u>by</u>.

e.g. He was surprised by/at her attitude.

(<u>Similar</u>: amazed at, astonished at)

k You rob/cure/deprive somebody <u>of</u> something.

l to go in search <u>of</u> something = to search <u>for</u> something

m to be fed up <u>with</u> ... = to be tired <u>of</u> ...

n <u>on principle</u> = as a matter of principle; <u>in principle</u> = in theory

o Note the following patterns: to differ <u>from</u>; to be different <u>from/to</u> (not <u>than</u>).

p We compare A <u>with</u> B to show their differences. A poet, however, will compare A <u>to</u> B as a simile or illustration. As a joining phrase, *compared* can be followed by either <u>with</u> or <u>to</u>.

e.g. Your house is luxurious compared with/to ours.

B

Task

Choose the correct alternative in brackets.

1 It took years of research, but (at / in) the end they found a cure for the disease.

2 He was eventually cured (from / of) the disease and was able to lead a normal life.

3 Everybody applauded (at / in) the end of the performance.

4 The audience was (comprised / composed / consisted) mainly of teenagers.

5 For him, happiness consists (of / in) having no responsibilities.

6 Cheese is made (of / from) milk.

7 I am not sure what this statue is made (of / from). Marble, I think.

8 Whilst the others slept, he set out in search (for / of) firewood and water.

9 There has been some improvement (in / on) his work.

10 This offer is certainly a vast improvement (in / on) their previous one.

11 (In / On) principle I agree (with / to) what you are saying, but we have to be realistic.

12 We managed to persuade him to agree (with / to) our request.

13 To be honest, I am surprised (at / by) her.

14 In the exam, the students were asked to compare the economy of post-war Japan (with / to) that of Italy.

15 Only you and (I / me) need know about this.

16 They want to come on holiday with my sister and (I / me).

17 My taste in music differs (from / to) hers.

18 It was different (to / than) what I had expected.

19 She said that she was fed up (with / of) her present job.

Score: /20

21

Regular verbs in the past

A

Each verb in brackets should end in -ed. As you change each verb, make any other necessary changes (e.g. doubling the last letter; changing y to i).

As Lieutenant Kowolski (sip) his coffee, he carefully (study) the man who was sitting opposite him. It was at times like these, he (admit) to himself, that he (envy) those officers who had (incur) the wrath of Captain Reilley and been (transfer) to traffic-control duties.

"Let's get this straight," (drawl) the lieutenant. "You say that this has (occur) more than once."

"Yes, sir," (reply) the man. "It has (happen) three times now."

"And each time, you say, you were (carry) off against your will."

"That is correct, officer. I (beg) them to let me go, but they (force) me to go with them. Naturally, I (offer) no resistance. That's why I wasn't (harm) physically."

"Why didn't you report the first incident?"

"They (order) me not to."

"I see. So, you have been (kidnap) three times."

"That's right, officer."

"By aliens, you say."

"Yes, sir. Creatures from outer space."

"And, each time, you (travel) to Mars and back in a cigar-shaped vessel. Is that correct?"

"That's correct, officer."

"Good heavens," (mutter) Lieutenant Kowolski.

Now check your answers and then consult the **Reference** section before going on to **B**.

Reference

a We use the suffix -ed to indicate the past form of a regular verb.

b If a one-syllable verb ends in a single vowel and consonant, we double the final consonant when we add -ed.

stop - stopped; fit - fitted; pat - patted; tap - tapped; hop - hopped

Exceptions: We never double the letters -w, -x, -y.

bow - bowed; fix - fixed; play - played

NB (i) If a verb already ends in -*e*, we just add -*d*.

e.g. hope - hoped; stare - stared

(ii) If a word ends in two vowels and a consonant, we do not double the final consonant.

e.g. steer - steered; peer - peered; fear - feared; pour - poured

c If a verb has more than one syllable and ends in a single vowel and consonant, we usually double the final consonant <u>if the last syllable is stressed</u>.

e.g. admit - admitted; prefer - preferred; occur - occurred

but offer - offered; open - opened; happen - happened; benefit - benefited; visit - visited

NB When considering words like *equip*, the letters *qu* count as a single consonant.

e.g. equip - equipped

Exceptions (1): handicap - handicapped; kidnap - kidnapped; worship - worshipped; program - programmed
(2): Even though the last syllable may not be stressed, we always double the -*l* when adding -*ed* to words ending in one vowel and -*l*.

e.g. travel - travelled; control - controlled

d If a verb ends in a consonant + -*y*, we change the *y* to *i* when we add -*ed*.

e.g. try - tried; cry - cried; carry - carried; hurry - hurried

e If a verb ends in -*ic*, we add *k* before -*ed*.

e.g. panic - panicked; picnic - picnicked

B

| Task 1 | Change each verb in brackets so that it ends in -*ed*.

He (apply) the brakes, but the car (skid) out of control. As it (veer) off the mountain road, he (panic) and desperately (try) to open the nearside door. To his horror, he (discover) that it was (jam). He was (trap)!
He (grit) his teeth and (steel) himself for the inevitable end. But just then ...

Score: /10

Change each verb in brackets so that it ends in -ed.

He (stare) at the old lady just ahead of him in the queue. He was certain
he (recognise) her. Wasn't she the actress who had (star) in 'Silver Moon'
some fifty years ago? He had (enjoy) that film very much and, like so
many boys of his generation, had (worship) the beautiful star as a
goddess.

He vaguely (recall) that she had (quarrel) with an important film
producer who had, subsequently, (cancel) her contract and, effectively,
(ruin) her career.

He (wonder) whether he should say something to her. Perhaps she
(prefer) not to be (remind) of the dim and distant past, of dreams that
had never been (fulfil).

As he (hesitate), a taxi (pull) up. Almost bent double and with the aid of
a walking stick, she (shuffle) forward. He (open) his mouth and …

Score: /17

22

Irregular verbs in the past

A

| Task |

Answer the questions below.

1 The past form of *bind* is *bound*. Can you think of three other verbs that follow the same pattern?

2 Look at the two sets of verbs below. Each set follows a common pattern in the past. What is the difference in pattern between set *a* and set *b*?
   a cling, fling, sting, swing, wring   b ring, sing, spring

3 Look at the following verbs: *bleed, breed, feed, flee, lead*. What common pattern do they follow in the past?

4 The verbs *lay* and *pay* share the same past form. What is it? Which other verb follows the same pattern in the past as these two verbs?

5 In terms of their past form, which two verbs are the odd ones out in the list of verbs below? Why?
   bet, burst, cast, cost, cut, dig, hit, hurt, let, put, quit, send, set, shed, spread, thrust

6 Three of the verbs below follow the same pattern in the past. Which one does not?
   swear, tear, hear, wear

7 *a* Which of the verbs below take *-ought* as their past form?
   b Which of the verbs below take *-aught* as their past form?
   bring, buy, catch, fight, seek, teach, think

8 Look at the two sets of verbs below. What common pattern does each set of verbs follow in the past?
   a mow, sew, show, sow   b draw, grow, know, throw

9 What common pattern do the verbs below follow when used in the past?
   begin, drink, run, shrink, sink, stink, swim

10 The past form of *weep* is *wept*. Can you think of four other verbs that follow the same pattern?

Now check your answers and then consult the **Reference** section before going on to **B**.

Reference

a As you have just seen in **A**, the majority of irregular verbs can be broken down into particular groups with their own pattern(s). It is easier to remember the past form(s) of the more difficult irregular verbs if you can relate them to other verbs that have a similar pattern. For example, *to strive* (past forms: strove, striven) is like *to drive* (drove, driven). Similarly, *to stride* (past forms: strode, stridden) is like *to ride* (rode, ridden).

b Some irregular verbs, however, cause particular spelling problems and/or do not fit readily into a convenient 'package'. These verbs should be learnt separately.

e.g.   bite (bit, bitten); break (broke, broken); choose (chose, chosen); forbid (forbade, forbidden); hide (hid, hidden); shake (shook, shaken); slide (slid); strike (struck); tread (trod, trodden); write (wrote, written)

c Particular attention should be paid to *lay* and *lie* as they are very confusing.
  ● The verb *to lay* (past form: laid) is a transitive verb. This means that it is always followed by an object noun or pronoun.

e.g.   The hen laid three eggs yesterday. / They have laid a new path in the front garden. / He laid down the law.

  ● The verb *to lie* (past forms: lay, lain) is an intransitive verb. This means that it does not take an object. It is usually followed by a preposition.

e.g.   We were told that the village lay in a picturesque valley. / She lay down and tried to sleep. / It had lain there for years.

  ● The verb *to lie* (past form: lied) means 'not to tell the truth'.

e.g.   I have never lied to you.

d When an irregular verb forms part of a compound verb, it changes in its usual way.

e.g.   see (saw, seen) - <u>foresee</u> (foresaw, foreseen); shine (shone) - <u>outshine</u> (outshone)

B

Task

Change each verb in brackets into an appropriate past form.

1   The Romans had a law that (forbid) the wearing of trousers.
2   They (strive) valiantly to keep the enemy at bay.
3   There was immediate silence when the headmaster (stride) into the hall.
4   She (lie) down on the sofa and tried to get a few minutes' sleep.
5   First she (lay) some newspapers over the kitchen floor and then she (begin) to paint the walls.
6   They asked him to play the song again, so he (rewind) the tape.

7   They were (show) to their seats by a very helpful usher.
8   Have you (mow) the lawn?
9   That particular advertisement has (mislead) a lot of people.

10 Not wishing to be (sting) by the wasps, he (fling) the jam
    sandwiches into the river.
11 As the fog (grow) thicker, the traffic (grind) to a halt.
12 The branch (strike) me in the face and (break) my nose.
13 In his final years, he (seek) solace in drink.
14 He (shake) his head in disbelief.
15 She (swim) to the life-raft and (cling) desperately to its side,
    but then a huge wave (sweep) her away and she was never
    (see) again.
16 The children (slide) happily down the muddy slope.
17 She (weep) openly when she (hear) the news.
18 Fearing that he would be (catch), the burglar (flee) empty-
    handed.
19 He (ring) the police after some boys had deliberately (tread) on
    his plants.
20 He (stink) of beer, and we were all absolutely disgusted.   Score: /30

23 Formal English

•••

A

| Task 1 |

Without changing its meaning, replace each underlined word with a more formal word.

1 I <u>would</u> like to take this opportunity to thank you all for your hard work.
2 You have raised an interesting point and I <u>will</u> certainly give it some thought.
3 "<u>Can</u> I leave the table?" the little boy asked politely.
4 I was shocked when Brian, <u>who</u> I had always considered to be my best friend, took Keith's side in the dispute.
5 The lawyer said that, <u>while</u> he sympathised with her point of view, he did not think that the situation warranted legal action.
6 In business, <u>you</u> should not allow <u>your</u> feelings to affect <u>your</u> judgement.

| Task 2 |

Make the sentences below more formal by changing the form of the underlined verbs.

1 I suggest that you <u>are</u> more careful in future.
2 It is vital that she <u>sees</u> a doctor immediately.

| Task 3 |

Rephrase the words that have been underlined without using *if.*

1 <u>If you should need</u> any further assistance, do not hesitate to contact me.
2 <u>If I had known</u> he was going to be there, I would not have gone.

Now check your answers and then consult the **Reference** section before going on to **B**.

Reference

a Traditionally, we conjugated the future tense in the following way: I *shall*, you will, he/she/it will, we *shall*, they will. In the same way, we conjugated the conditional tense as follows: I *should*, you would, he/she/it would, we *should*, they would.

Nowadays, *I/we will* and *I/we would* are perfectly acceptable in standard English. The traditional forms of the future and conditional tenses are still used, however, in formal English.

b In the past, we distinguished between *can* (denoting ability) and *may* (denoting permission). That distinction is no longer maintained rigidly in modern English. Between equals, it is more common to use *can* than *may* when asking or giving permission. In question form, *may* certainly sounds more polite than *can* – and should be used on formal occasions. In a statement, however, *may* often sounds cold, distant and officious. Official rules and regulations often contain the word *may*.

e.g. Students may not wear sandals on the premises.

c In formal written English, some writers prefer to follow the traditional rule that *who* changes to *whom* when it is the object of a verb.

e.g. 'We always love those who admire us, and we do not always love those whom we admire.' (La Rochefoucauld)

In modern English, it is perfectly acceptable to use *who* instead of *whom* when it is the object of the verb.

e.g. Who did you see? / Whom did you see? (very formal)

d *Whilst* and *amongst* are more formal than *while* and *among*.

e When talking in general, *one* is the formal equivalent of *you*. *One* can also be used in place of *I*.

f Note the following formal patterns:
- It is vital/essential that something (should) be done.
- to propose/suggest that something (should) be done.

g Conditional statements can be made more formal in the following ways:
- If I were rich ... = Were I rich ...
- If that were to happen ... = Were that to happen ...
- If he should need ... = Should he need ...
- If I had realised ... = Had I realised ...

B

| Task 1 |

Where possible, change *who* to *whom* in the sentences below. Tick any sentence where it is not possible to do so.

1 She was introduced to a man called Smith, who she vaguely recognised.
2 'The world tolerates conceit from those who are successful, but not from anybody else.' (John Blake)
3 'Almost all absurdity of conduct arises from the imitation of those who we cannot resemble.' (Samuel Johnson)

Score: /3

Task 2	Which of the following statements implies a clear distinction in status between the speaker and the person referred to?

1 "You may go," she said.
2 "You can use it any time you like," she said.   Score: /1

Task 3	Using formal English, fill in each gap with a suitable word.

I _____ be grateful if you could attend to this matter as soon as possible. _____ I known that there would be such a delay, I would never have contracted your company for the job. _____ I appreciate that you are not entirely to blame for some of the 'technical' difficulties that have arisen, the fact remains that you are two months behind schedule.

I _____ be away from the office for the next few days, and I trust that the matter will have been resolved by the time I return.

_____ does not wish to use threats, but I _____ like to remind you of the penalty clauses in the contract you signed.

_____ you require any further information with regard to our original specifications, please speak to Steven Hackney.   Score: /7

24 Emphatic English

A

Task

Finish each sentence in such a way that it means exactly the same as the sentence above it.

1. You must not touch those buttons under any circumstances.
   Under ...
2. They did not find out the truth until twenty years later.
   Not until ...
3. It is by no means certain that they will agree to our plan.
   By ...
4. Although I respect Renata very much, I do not think she is the right person for the job.
   Much ...
5. I know this may sound strange, but I don't really want to earn a lot of money.
   Strange ...
6. What impressed us most was their sincerity.
   It was ...
7. He lost everything because of his greed.
   It was ...

Now check your answers and then consult the **Reference** section before going on to **B**.

Reference

a. If you read poetry, you will have noticed that one way a poet achieves a dramatic effect is by inverting normal word order.

e.g.
Stormed at with shot and shell,
Boldly they rode and well,
Into the jaws of Death,
Into the mouth of Hell
Rode the six hundred.

(From *The Charge of the Light Brigade* by Alfred, Lord Tennyson)

b. Inversion is not just a device for poets. In normal prose, a number of adverbial words or phrases can be put at the beginning of a sentence for greater emphasis. These adverbial words/phrases include:

under no circumstances, on no account, not only, hardly, scarcely, no sooner, seldom, rarely, by no means, little, never, at no time, nowhere, not until, only, so, such

We use the question form of a verb after such adverbial expressions.

e.g. Little did he realise that he was being watched. / Never have I been so insulted!

NB (i) *Only* must be followed by a clause or phrase for inversion to take place.
(ii) After *only* and *not until*, inversion takes place in the second part of the sentence.

e.g. Not until I got home did I discover that my wallet was missing.
Only after I got home did I discover that my wallet was missing.

c As a more emphatic substitute for *although* + clause, we can use the following patterns: (i) *Much as* + subject + verb. (ii) Adjective + *as* + subject + verb.

e.g. Much as I like spaghetti, I don't want to eat it every day.
Poor as we are, we are by no means unhappy.

NB (i) *Much as* is used only with such personal verbs of feeling as *like, dislike, hate, admire, appreciate, (dis)approve, respect, sympathise, enjoy.*
(ii) After an adjective, we can use *though* instead of *as.*

e.g. Brilliant though he is, he cannot do simple arithmetic.

(iii) Note the following fixed phrase:

<u>Try as he might</u>, he could not get the car to start.

d The simplest way of clearly emphasising two parts of a sentence is to create a cleft (i.e. 'divided') sentence by the use of *it* and *that.*

e.g. <u>It was only when</u> he started speaking <u>that</u> I realised who he was.

B

| Task |

Finish each sentence in such a way that it means exactly the same as the sentence above it.

1 You will not find such generous and spontaneous hospitality anywhere else in the world.
Nowhere ...

2 The news was so shocking that nobody knew what to say.
So ...

3 We never suspected that the money had been stolen.
At no ...

4 They didn't tell me about it until later.
Only ...

5 It may seem strange, but he quite likes being in prison.
Strange ...

6   Although I sympathise with your point of view, I still feel you
    were wrong to do what you did.
    Much ...

7   Even though I admire her courage, I think it is foolish of her
    to go there on her own.
    Much ...

8   He may be good at languages, but he is hopeless at Maths.
    Good ...

9   Despite all his efforts, he could not force the door open.
    Try ...

10 Only after a long and violent struggle did they manage to
    subdue the prisoner.
    It was ...

Score: /10

Loose English

A

Do the sentences below make immediate sense when you read them? How can the sentences be improved?

1 Being Sunday, I didn't have to get up early.
2 Playing in the middle of the road, the car only just missed the two children.
3 Standing at the bus-stop, a gang of youths approached me and started threatening me.

Correct the sentences below.

1 "Would you mind if I use your bathroom?" she asked.
2 The reason why he is so tired is because he has not had a proper break for years.
3 She has a more interesting job than he does.
4 She can type faster than what I can.
5 France is three times larger than England.
6 She was sat by the window, reading a magazine.

Now check your answers and then consult the **Reference** section before going on to **B**.

Reference

a Look at the two sentences below. Each sentence begins with a participle clause.

Feeling tired and hungry, Rebecca asked if they could stop for a rest.
Founded in 1757, Ham School has a long and illustrious history.

A participle clause is formed with either a present participle (e.g. being, having) or a past participle (e.g. built, chosen), and is divided from the main clause by a comma. In the examples that you have just read, it is very clear that *Rebecca* is the subject of *feeling tired and hungry* and that *Ham School* is the subject of *founded in 1757*.

Now look at the following sentence:

Upset at the news, my mother tried to comfort me.

Who was upset? According to the sentence structure, it was *my mother*. Is that what the writer meant? In other words, the participle clause has been used too loosely and has created ambiguity.

When using a participle clause, make sure that the subject comes straight after the comma. Otherwise, you will end up with what is known as a 'dangling' participle.

b When using more than one verb, make sure that the tenses are in harmony.

e.g. <u>Do</u> you mind if I <u>open</u> a window? / <u>Would</u> you mind if I <u>opened</u> a window?

c Since *the reason* already contains the idea of *because*, there is no need to repeat the idea in the second part of a sentence. Use the following patterns:

The main reason is that ... / The reason (why) we are here today is that ... / The reason for the delay is that the pilot has been taken ill.

d We normally use *do* to avoid repeating a verb.

e.g. She works just as hard as he does.

In British English, this does not apply in the case of *to have* or *to be*.

e.g. She has her own point of view, just as he has.

e Be particularly careful with *what* and *than*. We do not use *what* after *than* except when *what* means 'that which / the things which'.

e.g. My younger brother can swim faster than I can.
This is better than what we ate yesterday.

f Note the following patterns:

The fish he caught this morning was <u>twice the size of</u> the one he caught last week.
The fish he caught this morning was <u>twice as big as</u> the one he caught last week.

Logically, we should follow the same pattern for *three times*, *four times*, etc.

e.g. The fish he caught this morning was <u>three times as big as</u> the one he caught last week.

g When describing where someone is seated, it is incorrect to say that someone *is sat* there.

In standard English, we should use the present participle (sitting) with *to be*.

e.g. I <u>was sitting</u> at my desk, doing my homework.

B

In only one of the sentences below has a participle clause been used correctly. Tick that sentence. How can the other sentences be improved?

1 Being sensible, I am sure that Katie will not do anything foolish.
2 Being such a miserable morning, we decided not to go to the beach.
3 Having been kept awake most of the night by the noise next door, Jessica was in a foul mood that morning.
4 Having suggested the idea in the first place, Mr Fowler could not understand why Ms Hodgkins had then objected to the plan.

Score: /4

Task 2

Finish each sentence in such a way that it means exactly the same as the sentence above it.

1 Her eyesight is better than mine.
  a She has ...
  b She can ...
2 The model aeroplane costs £10, whereas the model car costs £40.
  The model car is four ...
3 We are thinking of moving because we are not satisfied with any of the schools in our area.
  The reason ...
4 Do you mind if we postpone the meeting until tomorrow?
  Would it be all right if ...

Score: /5

Task 3

In which of the following sentences is there a mistake? Tick any sentence that is grammatically correct.

1 He's been sat there since eight o'clock this morning.
2 We sat at the back of the cinema.
3 She was sat in an armchair, knitting a jumper.
4 She sat next to me on the coach.

Score: /4

26   The comma and relative clauses

A

Task

Supply commas where necessary in the sentences below.

1   'Anthony Edwards has become television's highest-paid actor in a deal which ties him to the hospital drama ER for the next four years.

    Edwards who plays Dr Mark Greene has signed a £21 million contract: equivalent to almost £250,000 an episode.

    George Clooney who previously had the largest salary is leaving the series early next year.'

2   The Australian Aborigines were the earliest-known inhabitants of Australia. The term *aborigine* which comes from the Latin words *ab origine* means 'from the beginning'.

3   Australia is one of the world's leading exporters of sugar cane which is grown along the north-eastern coast.

4   The Arctic is dominated by the Arctic Ocean and a vast treeless plain called the tundra. Unlike Antarctica which is an ice-covered continent much of the Arctic consists of ice-covered seas.

5   The first successful animated cartoon with sound was *Steamboat Willie* (1928) which introduced the character Mickey Mouse.

Now check your answers and then consult the **Reference** section before going on to **B**.

Reference

a   A *relative clause* is a subordinate clause which gives more information about someone or something mentioned in the main clause. Relative clauses usually begin with a *relative pronoun* (e.g. that, which, who, whom, whose).

When considering the use of the comma with relative clauses, we need to bear in mind that there are two kinds of relative clause: *defining* and *non-defining*.

b A *defining* relative clause is one that identifies the person or thing being spoken about. Since this information is essential to the meaning of a sentence, no commas are used.

e.g. A farrier is a person *who shoes horses.*

The only mammal *that flies* is the bat.

If we took out the defining relative clauses, the sentences would clearly be incomplete.

c A *non-defining* relative clause gives further information about someone or something. We should think of a non-defining clause as an additional comment. We separate an additional comment from a main clause by means of the comma.

e.g. I am reading a book on graphology, *which is the study of handwriting.* The most popular vegetable in the world is the tomato, *which is used in more than 100 countries.*

If we took out the non-defining relative clauses, the sentences would still make perfect sense.

d Be careful when using the comma with a relative clause. When <u>enclosing</u> a relative clause within a main clause, make sure that you use two commas. Use one comma when the relative clause follows on from the main clause.

e.g. The whale shark, which may grow to be forty-five feet long and weigh fifty tons, is harmless. It eats very small animals, which it strains from the sea water.

B

Task

Supply commas where necessary in the sentences below. Tick any sentence that does not require commas.

1 'An actor is a sculptor who carves in snow.' (Lawrence Barrett)
2 'Man is the only animal that blushes. Or needs to.' (Mark Twain)
3 Henry VI who was only eight months old when he came to the throne in 1422 was England's youngest king.
4 The Dutch painter Van Meegeren who lived from 1899 to 1947 pulled off some of the most brilliant forgeries in art history.
5 Chess is a game that requires a great deal of concentration.
6 Unlike chess and draughts which are very ancient games the game of dominoes is comparatively new.
7 The first woman in space was Valentina Tereshkova of the former Soviet Union who orbited the Earth in June 1963.
8 Asia which occupies nearly one-third of the Earth's total land surface is the largest and most heavily populated of the world's continents.

9 The only British Prime Minister to have been assassinated was Spencer Perceval (1762–1812) who was shot dead when entering the lobby of the House of Commons.

10 The koala bear which eats nothing but eucalyptus leaves is one of the few land animals that do not need water to supplement their food.

11 Lake Baikal which is located in Siberia is the only lake in the world that is deep enough to have deep-sea fish.

12 Louis Pasteur whose work on wine, vinegar and beer led to pasteurisation had an obsessive fear of dirt and infection. He would never shake hands with anybody.

13 The introduction of pasteurisation which is a method of killing micro-organisms by heat has been a major factor in making milk safer to drink.

14 The German physicist Wilhelm Konrad Roentgen who discovered X-rays and initiated a scientific revolution in doing so refused to apply for any patents in connection with the discovery or to make any financial gain out of it. He died in poverty.

15 'That which is striking and beautiful is not always good; but that which is good is always beautiful.' (Ninon de l'Enclos)   Score: /15

The comma (general use)

A

| Task |

Supply commas where appropriate in the passage below.

The lawyer and the oyster

As two men were walking along the seashore they found an oyster and began to quarrel about it.

"I saw it first" said one of the men "so it belongs to me."

"I picked it up" said the other "so I have a right to keep it."

As they were quarrelling a lawyer came by and they asked him to decide for them in the matter.

The lawyer agreed to do so but before he would give his opinion he required the two men to give him their assurance that they would agree to whatever he decided.

Then the lawyer said "It seems to me that you both have a claim to the oyster; so I will divide it between you and you will then be perfectly satisfied."

Opening the oyster he quickly ate it and very gravely handed an empty shell to each of the men.

"But you have eaten the oyster!" cried the men.

"Ah that was my fee for deciding the case!" said the lawyer. "But I have divided all that remains in a perfectly fair and just manner."

That is what happens when two quarrelsome persons go to law about something that they cannot agree upon.

Now check your answers and then consult the **Reference** section before going on to **B**.

Reference

a The golden rule when using the comma is not to overuse it. If in doubt, omit it.

b We normally use the comma to make clear what is happening in a complex sentence. It is always best to mark off any subordinate clause from a main clause if the subordinate clause comes at the beginning of the sentence.

e.g.   Although the meeting lasted all day, no decisions were reached.

We should also mark off any subsidiary phrase, introductory word(s) or emphatic remark at the beginning of a sentence.

e.g. According to the doctors, there is little hope. | Incidentally, when will the report be ready? | Lord, hear our prayer.

c Generally speaking, it is best to place a comma after an adverb or adverbial phrase at the beginning of a sentence.

e.g. Sadly, the dog died shortly afterwards. | Miraculously, he survived the crash.

On the other hand, the structure/flow of a sentence may sometimes make it unnecessary or awkward to include a comma after an adverb or adverbial phrase.

e.g. Suddenly it began to pour down with rain and, not having an umbrella, I got completely soaked.

d Subordinate clauses and adjectival phrases that follow a main clause may also be marked off by a comma.

e.g. The waiter spilt some wine on my suit, completely ruining it. | I went to bed, tired but happy.

e When we join two independent clauses with a conjunction (e.g. and, but, or), we have the option of placing a comma before the conjunction if we feel it is necessary.

e.g. I wanted to book our tickets in advance, but the ticket-office was closed for the weekend.

f With direct speech, we use the comma in the following way:

e.g. He said, "Ah, yes, Mr Bond. Please come in."
"Please come in," he said. "I shall be with you in a moment."
"I am not sure," he said, "but I think it is on Wednesday."

g When using commas, you need to decide whether to use one comma (to mark off a division in a sentence) or two commas (to enclose an interruption within a sentence).

e.g. During most of the Middle Ages, few people were able to read or write. | During most of the Middle Ages, few people, including kings and emperors, were able to read or write.

h There are times when the grammar of a sentence demands the 'correct' use of the comma. More times than not, however, the use of the comma is a matter of personal preference and style.

B

Task

Supply commas where appropriate in the passage below.

When the steamship *Stella* left Southampton on the afternoon before Good Friday in the year 1899 she was bound for the Channel Islands with nearly two hundred passengers on board.
Not long after the ship had started her voyage the sea became

covered with fog. The captain hoped it would lift and kept the ship at full speed. But the fog grew thicker and the *Stella* crashed on some rocks. The lifeboats were lowered and the passengers behaved as bravely as men and women can in a crisis.

But the name of one woman will always be remembered when people think of the sinking of the *Stella*. Mrs Mary Rogers the stewardess comforted the women and gave each of them a life-belt fastening it with her own hands. She led them to the side of the sinking ship where the boats were being lowered. At the last moment it was found that one woman had no life-belt. Instantly the stewardess took off her own belt and gave it up and the woman was lifted safely into the boat. The sailors called to the stewardess to jump in but the boat was full.

"No no!" she said. "There is no room. One more and the boat will sink."

The ship sank into the sea and Mary Rogers looked on the world for the last time.

"Goodbye goodbye!" she cried and then: "Lord take me!"

Within a minute the *Stella* was gone and with her the brave stewardess.

Score: /15

28 The comma, the semicolon and the colon

* *

A

Task 1   In each sentence below, place a semicolon (;) where appropriate.

1 'Advice is seldom welcome and those who want it the most always like it the least.' (Lord Chesterfield)
2 Chess is one of the oldest games in the world so old in fact that no one knows who invented it.

Task 2   Use the comma and the semicolon where appropriate in the sentences below.

1 'When angry count to four when very angry swear.' (Mark Twain)
2 'To err is human to forgive divine.' (Alexander Pope)

Task 3   Use the comma and the colon (:) where appropriate in the sentences below.

1 The animal kingdom can be divided into two main groups those animals with a backbone (vertebrates) and those without a backbone (invertebrates).
2 I had the names and addresses of two of Beverley's friends a girl called Hannah Atkinson and a man called Terence Willows.

Now check your answers and then consult the **Reference** section before going on to **B**.

Reference

a The semicolon is stronger than a comma but weaker than a full stop. Sometimes two separate clauses are so closely related that we do not want to write them as separate sentences. In such cases, we can use the semicolon. Very often, there is a linking word or phrase before the second clause.

e.g.   I am sure he took it; in fact, I am positive he did.

Nobody really expected us to win; nevertheless, it was disappointing to lose.

b The semicolon can be used between two neatly balanced or contrasting statements.

'Forty is the old age of youth; fifty is the youth of old age.' (Victor Hugo)

Birds do not have teeth; they have beaks.

c Note the following uses:

- Normally we use commas to separate items in a list.

He bought a pair of socks, two shirts, a jacket and a tie.

- We use a colon if we wish to introduce a list of items.

The following items were stolen: a gold watch, a pen, a radio and some cutlery.

- We use a semicolon instead of a comma to group parts of a sentence that contains many commas.

For his daughter, he bought a dress; for his son, a watch; and for his wife, a silver bracelet.

d As well as introducing a list of items, the colon is used to introduce an example, a quotation or a direct explanation of what has just been stated.

The choice is clear: either we do as he says or we go to the police.

B

Task

Use the comma, the semicolon and the colon where appropriate in the sentences below.

1 Dualism underlies the condition of man. Every sweet has its sour every evil its good. For everything you have missed you have gained something and for everything you gain you lose something.   Score: /4

2 The reasons for her leaving the job were as follows first the unpleasant atmosphere in the office secondly there was little chance of promotion in the foreseeable future thirdly she was tired of working in a city and then there was the whole question of what she really wanted to do with her life.   Score: /7

3 'Society is composed of two great classes those who have more dinners than appetite and those who have more appetite than dinners.' (De Chamfort)   Score: /2

4 'Education makes a people easy to lead but difficult to drive easy to govern but impossible to enslave.' (Lord Brougham)   Score: /3

29   Unnecessary words

A

| Task |

Cross out any unnecessary words in the sentences below.

1   We were surrounded on all sides by thick, dense vegetation.
2   The atrocious weather was so awful that we decided to return back home.
3   He was unemployed and out of work for a period of three months.
4   Each and every student will receive a free complimentary copy of the magazine.
5   Despite his lack of experience, nevertheless he was offered the job.
6   Past experience has taught me not to mix business with pleasure.
7   As soon as you get home, please phone me immediately.
8   It was an issue that divided and split the Socialist Party.
9   It was not until ten years later that scientists appreciated the importance and significance of the discovery.
10   Her eyes literally shone like diamonds.

Now check your answers and then consult the **Reference** section before going on to **B**.

Reference

a   In spoken English, we use various devices to emphasise a word or phrase. One way of emphasising a point is to use different vocabulary to say the same thing twice.

e.g.   It was the right and proper thing to do.

A word or phrase which merely repeats the sense of a word or phrase that has just been used is a 'tautology' (unnecessary and usually unintentional repetition). In written English, the unnecessary repetition of a word or phrase should be avoided.

Over the years, various tautological expressions have crept into the English language and have become part of our normal vocabulary.

e.g.   null and void; prim and proper; peace and quiet

These are, however, fixed phrases. In your own writing, you should not create phrases of this type.

b   A common error in written English is to confuse a two-part verb with a verb that is complete in itself.

☒ We returned back to the hotel.

☑ We <u>went back</u> to the hotel.

☑ We <u>returned</u> to the hotel.

c Be careful not to use superfluous 'ornaments' in written English.

e.g. Past experience has taught me that one should not judge people by their appearance.

Since *experience* in this sentence clearly relates to the past, the word *past* is redundant.

d Look at the following two sentences:

a I was speaking in jest, but he took my words literally and was quite upset.

b My brother dashed out of the house and literally flew down the road.

- The first sentence would not make sense without the adverb *literally*. In the second sentence, however, *literally* does not make any sense as the verb *flew* is clearly being used in an imaginative or metaphorical way.
- The use of *literally* in the second sentence is an example of a common device used in spoken English. When employing *figurative* (imaginative/metaphorical) speech, we often use *literally* as an 'intensifier'. An intensifier is an adverb or adjective which adds emphasis to the word or phrase which follows it.

e.g. I am <u>very</u> happy.

Although common in spoken English, the use of *literally* as an intensifier should be avoided in written English.

- The adjective *actual* is another word that is often used as an intensifier in spoken English.

e.g. This is the actual dress worn by my grandmother when she got married.

Since *actual* means *real* or *current/present*, the word clearly has no meaning in the example above. This use of *actual* should be avoided in written English.

B

| Task | Cross out any unnecessary words in the sentences below.

1 She looked utterly and completely exhausted.
2 I am dreadfully and truly sorry about what happened the other day.

3 She asked her students to work in pairs of twos.

4 The student was told to rewrite the essay again.

5 The sheets were still slightly wet and damp.

6 There are two different kinds of speech: formal and informal speech.

7 He was asked whether he had ever taken illegal drugs at any time.

8 During the course of the race, two of the horses slipped and fell.

9 Personally I think that he has made the right decision.

10 When we got to the hotel, the manager was there in person to greet us.

11 Within a few weeks of being released from prison, he had reverted back to his old ways.

12 Therefore for that reason, I feel I have no option but to resign.

13 The coach departs at 6 a.m. in the morning.

14 He made so many mistakes and errors that the teacher told him to repeat the exercise again.

15 "What an unexpected surprise!" she exclaimed.

16 If you refer back to your notes, you will see that we have already covered that topic.

17 I rushed quickly down the stairs and opened the front door.

18 The car broke down and we had to walk the rest of the way on foot.

19 We asked him to keep the report as short and brief as possible.

20 The concert was so boring that the children yawned and fidgeted throughout the whole performance.

Score: /20

30   Plain English

A

Task 1

Below you will find six genuine examples of 'officially correct' language used by modern bureaucrats. In each case, what is being described? To help you decide, select your answers from the list given underneath (*a–j*). There are four extra words in the list.

1. 'A wheeled vehicle designed for the transport in a seated or semi-recumbent position of one or two babies who are placed inside a body of boat or box-like shape.'
2. 'Festive embellishments of an illuminary nature.'
3. 'A horticultural festive element.'
4. 'A grain-consuming unit.'
5. 'A domestic service engineer.'
6. 'An appliance for milling wooden dowels up to 10 millimetres in length.'

    a a Christmas tree *b* Christmas lights *c* a car *d* a pram
    e a tractor *f* a sheep, cow or pig *g* a housewife *h* a saw
    i a plumber *j* a pencil sharpener

Task 2

Below you will find some genuine examples of language used by modern business executives. What do all these statements mean in plain English?

1. "We are giving you a stimulated secondary opportunity to develop your career."
2. "We have decided to dehire you."
3. "You have been deselected."
4. "We are offering you accelerated retirement."
5. "We are downsizing your department."

Task 3

What do the words in italics mean? Rewrite them in plain English.

1. You can imagine my *chagrin* when I was not picked for the team.
2. And then he went upstairs for a nap, *as was his wont* on Sunday afternoons.
3. We had a marvellous holiday, *notwithstanding* the bad weather.
4. He inherited a *not inconsiderable* fortune.

Now check your answers and then consult the **Reference** section before going on to **B**.

Reference

a Nothing is gained by using unnecessarily complicated language. It will sound pompous and will usually be incomprehensible. Recently, a supermarket chain advertised for 'ambient replenishment assistants'. One could be forgiven for thinking that such a grandiose title denoted a highly skilled job. In fact, they were looking for people to stack shelves.

In the United States, the inability to speak a foreign language is officially labelled 'a negative dialogue capability situation'.

Such gobbledegook should be avoided at all times in your own writing.

b Try not to use 'big' words in order to impress the reader. The result often sounds pretentious.

e.g. We are endeavouring to ascertain her whereabouts. = We are trying to find out where she is.

c A 'euphemism' is a word or phrase that is gentler or less direct than the one normally used to refer to something unpleasant or embarrassing.

e.g. He has passed on/away. = He is dead.

Euphemisms have always been part of the English language. However, the modern trend of obsessively rephrasing anything that is remotely offensive or unpleasant has given rise to such expressions as 'a follicly challenged person' (= someone who is bald) and 'to subject a department to over-ratio amelioration' (= to reduce the number of staff in a department). The use of such ugly terminology is not recommended.

d When writing English, you should follow the advice given by Sir Ernest Gowers, the author of a very useful book, *The Complete Plain Words*: 'Be short, be simple, be human.'

B

Task

Just for fun, rephrase the following in plain English. Don't worry if you can't make head or tail of any of the sentences: it's not your fault.

1 How would you assess the dynamics of his interaction with his colleagues?
2 He shows little personal capacity for radical innovation.
3 Our company has at its core the mission of being one of the most flexible, cost-effective and high-quality suppliers of bureau services available. We are currently looking to employ proactive individuals to assist us in meeting this mission.

4 He is equipped with effective people management skills.
5 My father is a domestic refurbishment consultant.
6 Five people were outplaced when the Human Resources Department underwent a re-engineering process.
7 My brother is vertically challenged for his age.
8 I am afraid that, with regard to Mr Wilkins, we have a negative patient outcome.
9 The missile attack caused some collateral damage.

10 I have in mind to purchase a manual device for the purpose of fending off water precipitation occasioned by inclement meteorological conditions.

Answer key

Unit 1

A

Task 1 telephone, telegraph, telescope, microphone, microscope

Task 2 a
1 manuscript
2 manicure
3 manual
4 scripture(s)
5 We use the term *script* when we refer to the text of a play, film, broadcast or speech. We use the word when referring to a candidate's written answers in an exam. We also use the word when referring to a particular style or system of writing, e.g. Cyrillic script (used in some Slavonic languages).

b
1 prescription
2 inscription
3 description

B

Task 1 dictaphone, dictate, dictation, dictator, diction, dictionary, addict, contradict, edict, predict, verdict

Task 2 1 a proceeded b preceded c receded
2 *pre* = before; *re* = back; *pro* = forward/on
3 a exceed b concede c succeed
4 supersede (from the Latin *super* = over/above + *sedere* = to sit)

Unit 2

A

Task 1 1 retract
2 extract
3 subtract
4 attract
5 detract
6 distract
7 contract

Task 2 1 He/She is able to use both hands equally well.
2 It can be interpreted in more than one way.
3 It means you have mixed feelings (positive and negative).
4 *ambi* = both / on both sides

B

Task 1 A carnivore is an animal that eats meat. A herbivore is an animal that eats grass and other plants. An omnivore is able to eat both plants and meat.

Task 2 1 genocide   4 homicide
2 patricide   5 herbicide
3 suicide

Task 3 1 arch-rivals
2 pseudo-intellectual
3 hypersensitive
4 Claustrophobia
5 retrospect
6 foretell
7 anti-war
8 hyperactive
9 arachnophobia
10 pseudonym
11 retrograde
12 foregone

Unit 3

A

Task 1 1 *e*; 2 *b*; 3 *g*; 4 *a*; 5 *f*; 6 *i*; 7 *h*; 8 *c*; 9 *d*

Task 2 AD = in the year of Our Lord (used in the Christian calendar when referring to any year or century after Jesus Christ was born)
a.m. = before midday (in the morning)
e.g. = for example
etc. = and the rest / and so on
i.e. = that is
NB = note well
p.m. = after midday (afternoon/evening/night)
PS = postscript (used to introduce extra words added to the end of a letter or message)
RIP = (May he/she) rest in peace.

Task 3 1 rapport
2 coup
3 faux pas
4 cache
5 etiquette

B

Task 1 pneumonia - phenomenon - catastrophe - hippopotamus - psychology - confetti - graffiti - spaghetti - ghetto - yoghurt (or yogurt/yoghourt)

Task 2 chateaux - stimuli - radii - fungi - formulae - cacti - media - criteria - crises - oases

Task 3 1 *the status quo*: the present situation / the way things are
2 *bona fide* = genuine
3 *the pros and cons*: the arguments for and against something

Unit 4

A

Task 1 neighbour's behaviour
2 favourite colour
3 litre
4 licence
5 offence
6 acceptable
7 catalogue
8 axe
9 programme
10 acceptable
11 practised
12 practice

B

Task 1 humour
2 honour
3 theatre
4 acceptable
5 defence
6 acceptable
7 licensed
8 practice
9 acceptable
10 multicoloured/multi-coloured
11 meagre
12 dialogue
13 neighbourhood
14 centre
15 favourably
16 acceptable
17 favour
18 kilometres
19 armour
20 sombre

Unit 5

A

Task 1 ploughing   4 woollen
2 cheque   5 grey
3 travelled   6 tyre

7 skilfully
8 paralysed
9 enrol

10 marvellous
11 sceptical
12 anaesthetic

B

1 dialled
2 moustache
3 analysing
4 draught
5 pyjamas
6 jewellery

7 archaeologist
8 instalments
9 travelling
10 through
11 haemorrhage
12 equalled

Unit 6

A

Task

1 affect
2 adverse
3 illusion
4 appreciable
5 compliment
6 corpse
7 envelope

8 eminent
9 illicit
10 eluded
11 inquiry
12 explicit
13 humane
14 ingenious

B

Task

1 correct
2 effect
3 affecting
4 correct
5 adverse
6 illusion
7 appreciative
8 appreciable
9 complement
10 corps

11 correct
12 imminent
13 elicit
14 eludes
15 correct
16 correct
17 implicit
18 human
19 inhumane
20 ingenuous

Unit 7

A

Task infer, morale, respectfully, especially,
access, stationery, regrettable,
principal, loath, disinterested, later,
You're

B

Task

1 inferred
2 morale
3 respectively
4 regretful
5 specially
6 stationary
7 uninterested
8 principles
9 correct

10 loath/loth
11 principle
12 stationery
13 moral
14 implying
15 correct
16 especially
17 latter

Unit 8

A

Task

1 past
2 whether
3 pale
4 fir
5 soul
6 bough
7 site
8 software
9 prise
10 formally
11 wry
12 poured
13 grateful

B

Task 1

1 dependent
2 councillor
3 hoard
4 whet
5 playwright

Task 2

1 lifebuoys/life-buoys, quayside,
   threw
2 taught, knead, dough, bread
3 sure, its, paw, great, pain
4 muscles, beach
5 They're, their, there
6 too (far), hear
7 whole, mourning, died
8 piece, steak, plaice

Unit 9

A

Task
1 I *received a lot of / plenty of* presents *from* my cousins.
2 I asked him where he had *stolen* all *those things/items* from.
3 He *cheated* me out of £10.
4 It's *fortunate* we booked our tickets early.
5 I usually have a bath *just* before I go to bed.
6 *If* you won the lottery, what would you do?
7 The test was *very* easy.
8 She's *rather arrogant*.
9 You should *stand* up for your principles.
10 She told him to *keep* to the point.
11 He *became* really *angry* when I told him he had to *make/prepare* his own dinner for once.
12 He asked us to wait for *a while*.

B

Task 1
1 at all / in the least
2 quite/rather
3 a slight headache
4 a slight argument
5 slightly / a little
6 to pieces
7 a large amount of
8 very pleased/excited; absolutely thrilled
9 scrap/piece
10 part/end

Task 2
1 became, was
2 struck/hit
3 seized/took
4 started/began
5 understand
6 implying / trying to say
7 achieve nothing
8 becomes too/very excited and forgets herself; becomes over-excited

9 annoys/irritates
10 almost/nearly
11 returns, manages / has the chance/opportunity
12 affect, fetch/bring

Task 3
1 was furious/very angry
2 lost her nerve
3 bankrupt
4 threw
5 give up / resign from
6 much less / let alone
7 a great deal of
8 think, mad/crazy/insane
9 cheated him

Unit 10

A

Task
1 *There are* plenty of things that you can do.
2 You should *have* told me earlier.
3 When he was questioned by the police, he said he hadn't seen *anything* (or ... he *had* seen nothing).
4 *Barry and I* went swimming on Saturday.
5 We went (down) *to* the park for a game of football.
6 I thought he would find the test very difficult, but he did it *really quickly* and without a single mistake.
7 My mother and I *were* walking down the road when we heard a loud shriek behind us.
8 If I *were* you, I would see a doctor.
9 *As* I've said before, I don't see why I should help her.
10 Trevor definitely took the money. I *saw* him do it.

Task	1	He looked *as if/though* he needed a holiday.
	2	correct
	3	She looked *as if/though* she had been crying.
	4	She acted *as if/though* she owned the place.
	5	We went to Brighton, *as* we do every year.
	6	If I had been in his position, I would *have* done exactly what he *did*.
	7	You might *have* told me you had invited an extra twenty people to the party!
	8	They searched the whole house, but they didn't find *anything (or … they *found* nothing) incriminating.
	9	He said that he hardly *ever* went out in the evenings.
	10	The teacher said that she did not want to hear *any* more noise.
	11	They were sitting quite *happily* in the car.
	12	correct
	13	He looked *anxiously* at his watch.
	14	*There are* usually a lot more accidents on the motorways when it is foggy.
	15	If I *were* the headteacher of this school, I would abolish homework.
	16	My sister works *at* the local supermarket.
	17	My brother and I *were* putting up our tent when a sudden gust of wind blew it away.
	18	Everybody in the class *was* interested when I suggested an end-of-term party.
	19	He *doesn't* know what he's talking about.
	20	As he *began* to speak, the doorbell rang.

Unit 11

A

Task	1	It's not the cost *that* worries me, it's the time it will take.
	2	It was the way he dealt with the problem *that* impressed us most.
	3	The people *who* live in the cottage opposite us are not very friendly.
	4	"My daughter's happiness is all *that* matters," he said.
	5	"I need to buy a birthday card," she said. "For *whom*?" he asked.
	6	He is someone in *whom* I have complete faith.
	7	It's no use *my* telling him. He never listens to me.
	8	Excuse *my* asking, but are you wearing a wig?
	9	He said he would show me *a quicker way* of doing it.
	10	*Fewer* than a hundred people attended the concert.
	11	No sooner had I watered the plants in the garden *than* it began to rain.
	12	I have never *done* and would never do such a thing!

B

Task		NB Any answer in brackets means that it can be omitted without affecting the grammar of the sentence.
	1	My mother doesn't like the idea of *my* travelling abroad on my own.
	2	The only thing (*that*) I don't like about her is that she can be a bit bossy at times.
	3	correct
	4	You won't meet *a nicer* person than Daksha.
	5	No sooner had she entered the room *than* everyone started clapping and cheering.

6 correct

7 Everything (*that*) she said was absolutely true, and I told her so.

8 There have been *fewer* accidents on this stretch of the motorway since the introduction of speed traps.

9 *To whom* shall I address this letter?

10 I am afraid (*that*) there is very little possibility of *his* passing the exam.

11 The police wanted to know *from whom* we had obtained the information.

12 correct

13 She objected to *my* smoking in her house.

14 It was the discovery of an enormous hole over the South Pole *that* made people aware of the damage being done to the ozone layer.

15 He's been making *fewer* spelling mistakes since he started attending Mr Brown's class.

16 "Those are not the shoes (*that*) I ordered," he said.

17 *To whom* does this belong? or *Who* does this belong *to*?

18 They didn't offer him the job, despite *his* being a competent carpenter and joiner.

19 correct

20 I have always *followed* and will always follow my instincts in such matters.

5 a solicitor
6 a lawyer
7 a radiator
8 an announcer
9 a spectator
10 a caterpillar
11 a liar
12 a doctor
13 a sailor
14 a collar
15 a dictator
16 a prisoner
17 a visitor
18 a word-processor
19 an author
20 a burglar

B

Task 1
1 a survivor
2 a beggar
3 an inspector
4 vinegar
5 an editor
6 a gardener
7 a governor
8 a ventilator
9 a computer
10 a thermometer

Task 2
1 Conqueror
2 director, conductor, actors
3 transistor
4 objectors
5 inventor
6 explorer, navigator
7 calendar
8 Emperor, competitor

Unit 12

A

Task
1 a translator
2 a smuggler
3 grammar
4 a traitor

Unit 13

A

Task
1 eloquence
2 importance
3 Appearances
4 convenience

5 correspondence
6 alliance
7 assistance
8 coincidence
9 innocence
10 violence
11 Resistance
12 independence
13 confidence
14 appliance
15 relevance, evidence

B

Task 1
1 disappearance
2 reassurance
3 hindrance
4 Remembrance
5 maintenance
6 admittance
7 excellence

Task 2
1 Absence
2 acquaintance
3 repentance
4 endurance
5 substance
6 Silence
7 influence
8 performances
9 experience
10 difference
11 conference, audience, ignorance

Unit 14

A

Task
1 laboratory
2 battery
3 vocabulary
4 bravery
5 injury
6 necessary
7 unsatisfactory
8 cemetery
9 voluntary

10 slippery
11 military
12 machinery, factory
13 directory
14 missionary
15 stationery

B

Task
1 dictionary
2 library
3 advisory
4 confectionery
5 primary
6 February
7 temporary
8 compulsory
9 summary
10 itinerary
11 perjury
12 memory
13 extraordinary
14 victory
15 anniversary
16 secretary
17 solitary
18 predatory
19 scenery
20 adultery
21 tributary
22 estuary
23 contrary
24 Hungary
25 hereditary
26 territory
27 lavatory

Unit 15

A

Task
1 anxious
2 ferocious
3 generous
4 ambitious
5 ludicrous

6 courteous
7 self-conscious
8 notorious
9 pompous
10 religious
11 delicious
12 virus
13 outrageous
14 atrocious
15 spontaneous

B

Task 1
1 humorous
2 monstrous
3 hilarious
4 malicious
5 mischievous
6 furious
7 mysterious
8 vigorous
9 courageous
10 spacious

Task 2
1 fictitious
2 contagious
3 oblivious
4 octopus
5 vicious
6 suspicious
7 hideous
8 luxurious
9 previous
10 instantaneous
11 pretentious
12 conscientious

Unit 16

A

Task 1
1 forty
2 ninth
3 twelfth
4 explanation
5 exclamation
6 revelation
7 repetition
8 height

Task 2
1 surprised, knowledgeable
2 beginning, noticeable
3 exciting, disappointing
4 desperate, environment
5 irresponsible, unforgivable

B

Task 1
1 incurable
2 irreconcilable
3 unforgettable
4 unmistakable
5 indescribable
6 irreplaceable
7 unpalatable

Task 2
1 proclamation, government
2 separate, entrance
3 pronunciation
4 irrational, irrelevant
5 disapproval
6 illogical, illegible
7 ninety-nine
8 cancellation
9 dissatisfied
10 twentieth

Unit 17

A

Task 1
1 accidentally
2 domestically, specially
3 no mistakes
4 happily
5 recklessly
6 incredibly
7 gently
8 possibly
9 no mistakes
10 cheerfully

Task 2
The problem here is the position of *badly* in *b*. In *a* the adverb clearly qualifies *needs*. In *b*, however, the position of the adverb creates an ambiguous statement.

In *a*, the speaker is merely expressing some reservation. In *b*, the speaker is clearly emphasising that she *does not want* to go there.

Task 4   *b*: He asked me *to* carefully *note down* ...

B

Task   1   He responded sympathetically to her request.
2   They argue occasionally, like all couples.
3   He said that they had to surrender unconditionally.
4   She behaved unpredictably.
5   I had originally planned to have a very quiet wedding.
6   His proposal was heavily criticised by everybody concerned.
7   They struggled heroically against impossible odds.
8   He was fatally injured.
9   The fire was probably caused by an electrical fault.
10   She died peacefully.
11   The cost of petrol has risen dramatically.
12   They suffered terribly.
13   She, very sensibly, called the police. (Alternatively, we could say: Very sensibly, she called the police.)
14   He looked angrily at her. / He looked at her angrily.
15   Although he apologised profusely, she would not forgive him.

Unit 18

A

Task   1   flair
2   afflicts
3   broach
4   emigrate
5   bated
6   flouting
7   filing
8   sometime
9   left
10   luxuriant
11   heroin

B

Task   1   inflicted
2   some time, sometime
3   filing
4   flare
5   forgotten, left
6   brooch
7   flaunt
8   flair
9   baited
10   sometime
11   inflict
12   luxurious
13   heroine
14   baiting
15   afflicted
16   flout

Unit 19

A

Task 1   1   authoritarian
2   emotive
3   definitive
4   odious
5   exotic
6   contemptible
7   deceased
8   effective
9   deficient
10   urban
11   blond
12   quite, dessert

Task 2	1	non-flammable
	2	series
	3	unawares

B

Task	1	emotional
	2	authoritarian
	3	contemptible
	4	diseased
	5	efficient
	6	urbane
	7	defective
	8	desert, unawares
	9	inflammable
	10	definitive, authoritative
	11	emotive
	12	odious
	13	erotic
	14	contemptuous
	15	deceased

Unit 20

A

Task 1	1	Please keep this to yourself. This is strictly between you and *me*.
	2	The new committee will *consist of* / *comprise* ten members: seven students and three teachers.
	3	For me, the beauty of this poem consists *in* its unusual imagery.
	4	Glass is made *from* sand.
	5	The criminal's plan was to substitute fake diamonds *for* the ones he intended to steal.
	6	You have got away with it so far, but they will catch you *in* the end.

Task 2	1	to
	2	on
	3	at
	4	of
	5	of
	6	with
	7	on

| | 8 | from/to |
| | 9 | to |

B

Task	1	in
	2	of
	3	at
	4	composed
	5	in
	6	from
	7	of
	8	of
	9	in
	10	on
	11	In, with
	12	to
	13	at
	14	with
	15	I
	16	me
	17	from
	18	to
	19	with

Unit 21

A

| Task | sipped, studied, admitted, envied, incurred, transferred, drawled, occurred, replied, happened, carried, begged, forced, offered, harmed, ordered, kidnapped, travelled, muttered |

B

| Task 1 | applied, skidded, veered, panicked, tried, discovered, jammed, trapped, gritted, steeled |

| Task 2 | stared, recognised, starred, enjoyed, worshipped, recalled, quarrelled, cancelled, ruined, wondered, preferred, reminded, fulfilled, hesitated, pulled, shuffled, opened |

Unit 22

A

Task 1 find (found); grind (ground); wind (wound)

2 The verbs in set *a* have one past form (-*ung*): cling (clung); fling (flung); sting (stung); swing (swung); wring (wrung). The verbs in set *b* have two past forms (-*ang*, -*ung*): ring (rang, rung); sing (sang, sung); spring (sprang, sprung). NB If a verb has two past forms, the first one is used to indicate the simple past and the second one is used as a past participle.

3 They share the same past form (-*ed*): bleed (bled); breed (bred); feed (fed); flee (fled); lead (led).

4 lay (laid); pay (paid); say (said)

5 Two verbs in the list have separate past forms: dig (dug), send (sent). The others do not change in the past.

6 The three verbs that share a common pattern are: swear (swore, sworn); tear (tore, torn); wear (wore, worn). The past form of *hear* is *heard*.

7 *a* bring (brought); buy (bought); fight (fought); seek (sought); think (thought). *b* catch (caught); teach (taught)

8 *a* mow (mow*ed*, mow*n*); sew (sew*ed*, sew*n*); show (show*ed*, shown); sow (sow*ed*, sow*n*). *b* draw (dr*ew*, drawn); grow (gr*ew*, grown); know (kn*ew*, known); throw (thr*ew*, thrown)
NB Some people regard the verbs in group *a* as regular verbs and use -*ed* for the past participle.

9 These verbs have two past forms. The simple past form is spelt with an *a*, and the past participle is spelt with a *u*: begin (began, begun); drink (drank, drunk); run (ran, run); shrink (shrank, shrunk); sink (sank, sunk); stink (stank, stunk); swim (swam, swum). Note also the examples in 2*b* above.

10 creep (crept); keep (kept); sleep (slept); sweep (swept)

B

Task 1 forbade
2 strove
3 strode
4 lay
5 laid, began
6 rewound
7 shown
8 mown
9 misled
10 stung, flung
11 grew, ground
12 struck, broke
13 sought
14 shook
15 swam, clung, swept, seen
16 slid
17 wept, heard
18 caught, fled
19 rang, trodden
20 stank

Unit 23

A

Task 1 1 should
2 shall
3 May
4 whom
5 whilst
6 one, one's, one's

Task 2 1 I suggest that you *be* more careful in future.

2 It is vital that she *see* a doctor immediately.

Task 3 1 Should you need ...
2 Had I known ...

B

Task 1 1 She was introduced to a man called Smith, *whom* she vaguely recognised.
2 no change
3 'Almost all absurdity of conduct arises from the imitation of those *whom* we cannot resemble.'

Task 2 The first statement.

Task 3 should, Had, Whilst, shall, One, should, Should

Unit 24

A

Task 1 Under no circumstances must you touch (*or* ... are you to touch) those buttons.
2 Not until twenty years later did they find out the truth.
3 By no means is it certain that they will agree to our plan.
4 Much as I respect Renata, I do not think she is the right person for the job.
5 Strange as/though this may sound, I don't really want to earn a lot of money.
6 It was their sincerity that impressed us most.
7 It was because of his greed that he lost everything.

B

Task 1 Nowhere else in the world will you find such generous and spontaneous hospitality.

2 So shocking was the news that nobody knew what to say.
3 At no time did we suspect that the money had been stolen.
4 Only later did they tell me about it.
5 Strange as/though it may seem, he quite likes being in prison.
6 Much as I sympathise with your point of view, I still feel you were wrong to do what you did.
7 Much as I admire her courage, I think it is foolish of her to go there on her own.
8 Good as/though he may be at languages, he is hopeless at Maths.
9 Try as he might, he could not force the door open.
10 It was only after a long and violent struggle that they managed to subdue the prisoner.

Unit 25

A

Task 1 1 It being Sunday / Since it was Sunday / As it was Sunday, I didn't have to get up early.
2 The car only just missed the two children who were playing in the middle of the road.
3 I was standing at the bus-stop when a gang of youths approached me and started threatening me. / Standing at the bus-stop, I was approached by a gang of youths who started threatening me.

Task 2 1 "Would you mind if I *used* your bathroom?" she asked. / "*Do* you mind if I use your bathroom?" she asked.
2 The reason (why) he is so tired is

that he has not had a proper break for years.

3 She has a more interesting job than he *has*.

4 She can type faster *than I can*.

5 France is three times *as large as* England.

6 She was *sitting* by the window, reading a magazine.

B

Task 1

1 Katie is sensible, so I am sure that she will not do anything foolish. / Being a sensible girl/person/child, Katie will not do anything foolish.

2 Since/As it was such a miserable morning, we decided not to go to the beach.

3 correct

4 Since/As Ms Hodgkins had suggested the idea in the first place, Mr Fowler could not understand why she had then objected to the plan.

Task 2

1 *a* She has better eyesight than I have.
   b She can see better than I can.

2 The model car is four times as expensive as the model aeroplane.

3 The reason (why) we are thinking of moving is that we are not satisfied with any of the schools in our area.

4 Would it be all right if we postponed the meeting until tomorrow?

Task 3

1 *sitting* not *sat*
2 correct
3 *sitting* not *sat*
4 correct

Unit 26

A

Task

1 'Anthony Edwards has become television's highest-paid actor in a deal which ties him to the hospital drama *ER* for the next four years.
Edwards, who plays Dr Mark Greene, has signed a £21 million contract: equivalent to almost £250,000 an episode.
George Clooney, who previously had the largest salary, is leaving the series early next year.'

2 The Australian Aborigines were the earliest-known inhabitants of Australia. The term *aborigine*, which comes from the Latin words *ab origine*, means 'from the beginning'.

3 Australia is one of the world's leading exporters of sugar cane, which is grown along the north-eastern coast.

4 The Arctic is dominated by the Arctic Ocean and a vast treeless plain called the tundra. Unlike Antarctica, which is an ice-covered continent, much of the Arctic consists of ice-covered seas.

5 The first successful animated cartoon with sound was *Steamboat Willie* (1928), which introduced the character Mickey Mouse.

B

Task

1 no commas needed
2 no commas needed
3 Henry VI, who was only eight months old when he came to the throne in 1422, was England's youngest king.

4   The Dutch painter Van Meegeren, who lived from 1899 to 1947, pulled off some of the most brilliant forgeries in art history.

5   no commas needed

6   Unlike chess and draughts, which are very ancient games, the game of dominoes is comparatively new.

7   The first woman in space was Valentina Tereshkova of the former Soviet Union, who orbited the Earth in June 1963.

8   Asia, which occupies nearly one-third of the Earth's total land surface, is the largest and most heavily populated of the world's continents.

9   The only British Prime Minister to have been assassinated was Spencer Perceval (1762–1812), who was shot dead when entering the lobby of the House of Commons.

10 The koala bear, which eats nothing but eucalyptus leaves, is one of the few land animals that do not need water to supplement their food.

11 Lake Baikal, which is located in Siberia, is the only lake in the world that is deep enough to have deep-sea fish.

12 Louis Pasteur, whose work on wine, vinegar and beer led to pasteurisation, had an obsessive fear of dirt and infection. He would never shake hands with anybody.

13 The introduction of pasteurisation, which is a method of killing micro-organisms by heat, has been a major factor in making milk safer to drink.

14 The German physicist Wilhelm Konrad Roentgen, who discovered X-rays and initiated a scientific revolution in doing so, refused to apply for any patents in connection with the discovery or to make any financial gain out of it. He died in poverty.

15 no commas needed

Unit 27

A

Task   NB Commas indicated in brackets (,) are optional.

As two men were walking along the seashore, they found an oyster and began to quarrel about it.

"I saw it first," said one of the men, "so it belongs to me."

"I picked it up," said the other, "so I have a right to keep it."

As they were quarrelling, a lawyer came by(,) and they asked him to decide for them in the matter. The lawyer agreed to do so, but before he would give his opinion he required the two men to give him their assurance that they would agree to whatever he decided.

Then the lawyer said, "It seems to me that you both have a claim to the oyster; so I will divide it between you, and you will then be perfectly satisfied."

Opening the oyster, he quickly ate it and(,) very gravely(,) handed an empty shell to each of the men.

"But you have eaten the oyster!" cried the men.

"Ah, that was my fee for deciding the case!" said the lawyer. "But I have divided all that remains in a perfectly fair and just manner."

That is what happens when two quarrelsome persons go to law about something that they cannot agree upon.

B

Task

NB Commas indicated in brackets (,) are optional.

When the steamship *Stella* left Southampton on the afternoon before Good Friday in the year 1899, she was bound for the Channel Islands(,) with nearly two hundred passengers on board.

Not long after the ship had started her voyage, the sea became covered with fog. The captain hoped it would lift, and kept the ship at full speed. But the fog grew thicker(,) and the *Stella* crashed on some rocks. The lifeboats were lowered(,) and the passengers behaved as bravely as men and women can in a crisis.

But the name of one woman will always be remembered when people think of the sinking of the *Stella*. Mrs Mary Rogers, the stewardess, comforted the women and gave each of them a life-belt, fastening it with her own hands. She led them to the side of the sinking ship, where the boats were being lowered. At the last moment(,) it was found that one woman had no life-belt. Instantly(,) the stewardess took off her own belt and gave it up, and the woman was lifted safely into the boat. The sailors called to the stewardess to jump in, but the boat was full.
"No, no!" she said. "There is no room. One more and the boat will sink."

The ship sank into the sea, and Mary Rogers looked on the world for the last time.

"Goodbye, goodbye!" she cried, and then: "Lord, take me!"

Within a minute the *Stella* was gone, and with her the brave stewardess.
(Score: deduct one mark per mistake)

Unit 28

A

Task 1

1 'Advice is seldom welcome; and those who want it the most always like it the least.'

2 Chess is one of the oldest games in the world; so old in fact that no one knows who invented it.

Task 2

1 'When angry, count to four; when very angry, swear.'

2 'To err is human; to forgive, divine.'

Task 3

1 The animal kingdom can be divided into two main groups: those animals with a backbone (vertebrates), and those without a backbone (invertebrates).

2 I had the names and addresses of two of Beverley's friends: a girl called Hannah Atkinson, and a man called Terence Willows.

B

Task

1 Dualism underlies the condition of man. Every sweet has its sour; every evil its good. For everything you have missed, you have gained something; and for everything you gain, you lose something.

2 The reasons for her leaving the job were as follows: first, the unpleasant atmosphere in the office; secondly, there was little chance of promotion in the foreseeable future; thirdly, she was tired of working in a city; and then there was the whole question of what she really wanted to do with her life.

3 'Society is composed of two great classes: those who have more dinners than appetite, and those who have more appetite than dinners.'

4 'Education makes a people easy to lead, but difficult to drive; easy to govern, but impossible to enslave.'

Unit 29

A

1 Omit *on all sides*. Omit *thick* or *dense* and the comma.
2 Omit *atrocious* and *back*.
3 Omit *and out of work* and *a period of*.
4 Omit *and every*. Omit *free* or *complimentary*.
5 Omit *nevertheless*.
6 Omit *Past*.
7 Omit *immediately*.
8 Omit *and split*.
9 Omit *and significance*.
10 Omit *literally*.

B

Task 1 Omit *and completely*.
2 Omit *and truly*.
3 Omit *of twos*.
4 Omit *again*.
5 Omit *and damp*.
6 Omit *different* and the final word (*speech*).
7 Omit *at any time*.
8 Omit *the course of* and, if you wish, *of the* before *horses*.
9 Omit *Personally*.
10 Omit *in person*.
11 Omit *back*.
12 Omit *for that reason*.
13 Omit *in the morning*.
14 Omit *and errors* and *again*.
15 Omit *unexpected* and change *an* to *a*.
16 Omit *back*.
17 Omit *quickly*.
18 Omit *on foot*.
19 Omit *and brief*.
20 Omit *whole*.

Unit 30

A

Task 1 | 1 *d*; 2 *b*; 3 *a*; 4 *f*; 5 *g*; 6 *j*
Task 2 | All five statements mean "You are fired!".
Task 3 | 1 disappointment/annoyance
2 as he usually did
3 despite / in spite of
4 large

B

Task 1 How well does he get on with his colleagues?
2 He shows little initiative. / He is not very creative.
3 As suppliers of bureau services, our company's aim is to be one of the best in the field. We are seeking capable individuals to help us fulfil this aim.
4 He is a good manager.
5 My father is a furniture salesman.
6 Five people lost their jobs when the Personnel Department was re-organised.
7 My brother is short for his age.
8 I am afraid that Mr Wilkins has died.
9 Innocent civilians died as a result of the missile attack.
10 I am thinking of buying an umbrella.

Printed in the United States
By Bookmasters